ABOUT THE AUTHOR

William R. (Bill) Kaufmann continues to have a full and meaningful career. He has experienced and held leadership positions in all sectors of for-profit, non-profit and the public sectors in the following capacities:

- National and International coach/consultant
- William & Mary Adjunct Professor
- Columnist
- Corporate Executive
- President, Entrepreneurial companies
- Executive Recruiter

Taken one by one, the following is an overview summary:

- **National and International coach/consultant** – The primary focus centered on "The Management of Change" in the form of: Acquisitions/Mergers, Strategic Redirection, Turnaround, Accelerated Growth and Performance Improvement. A partial list of companies, both public and private are: SmithKline Beecham, BlueCross/Blue Shield of Virginia, ESAB, Warner-Lambert/Parke Davis, Spalding, among 20 others

- **Coaching/consulting to non-profit or public sector organizations** – Projects include reorganization of the State of New Jersey Judiciary, AIPAC a national lobbying group, the City of Williamsburg, Chamber of Commerce/Convention and Visitors Bureau, Williamsburg Landing - a CCRC, Hotel/Motel Association, and so on.

- **The College of William & Mary** – Taught Merger/Acquisition Integration and Organization Behavior at the MBA level; Organized Executive Partners: Grew from 4 to 120 retired and semi-retired executives over the past 14 years, to mentor MBA and undergraduate business school students at the Mason School of Business, in classroom, consulting and job preparation activities.

- **Columnist** – Write for the Virginia Gazette, one of the oldest continuous newspapers in America, on the steps and content skills and understanding for a job search strategy. This column is for talented people who are having difficulty finding a satisfying and contributive position in an organization for which they are comfortably matched.

- **Corporate executive** – President, Vice President and Director for businesses moving through major change, from major corporations like Questor, Chemlawn, American Optical and so on, to entrepreneurial companies like Williamsburg Partners, Williamsburg Fabricators, to name a few.

- **Executive Recruiter** – Recruited top executives of for-profit and non-profit organizations including Presidents, Vice-Presidents, Directors and functions of Chief Financial Officer, Marketing, Human Resources, Training & Development, Communications & Public Relations, Compensation & Benefits and Field Services.

Bill has taken all of these broad and deep experiences to compress them into a workbook for talented individuals to understand and apply in practical steps how to design and implement a compelling job search strategy. It's the reason why **FINDING A JOB: A HANDBOOK OF THE BEST JOB SEARCH STRATEGIES FOR SUCCESS** was written and is so powerful. To date, Bill has a 91% success rate with his clients.

FOREWORD:

A SENIOR EXECUTIVE SAYS:

"As a senior executive of international corporations, I have experienced thousands of hiring situations where the applicants are all qualified, but only one or two become candidates. Why? Because these few understand the preparation, skills and experiences that go into an effective job search strategy.

My Greener Future is an outstanding resource for those in the job market and smart enough to seek out expert counsel. Bill Kaufmann, being a professional with 40 years experience, has captured the "insider's handbook" of a successful job search. It's worth your time and effort to learn what he has to offer.

As an aside, I use Bill's insights to guide and mentor students and people I work with for their job searches. I encourage you to read and apply the content of this handbook. Let Bill help you succeed."

Robert R. Taylor, Former Vice President, Reebok International, Ltd

SATISFIED AND SUCCESSFUL CUSTOMERS SAY:

- **"My Greener Future gave me a direction that changed my life"**
  Sharon R., Salt Lake City, Utah

- **"I thought I knew how to market myself. I didn't. Bill is a true master of his craft!", Rich K., Virginia**

- **"My resume went from blah to eye-popping!"**

- **"In today's tough economy, I couldn't afford NOT to hire Bill!"**

- **"Outstanding program that I would recommend to anyone", Pat M, Ohio**

- **"Bill saw my future before I did. I'm currently achieving my dream!", Mary in Ohio**

- **"My Greener Future helped me enter a new and exciting career direction"**
  Chris in Jacksonville, Florida

- **"Individualized 'coaching' toward the art of marketing yourself.... Priceless.", Ken A., Chesterfield, Va.**

TABLE OF CONTENTS

HOW TO CONTACT BILL KAUFMANN FOR ADDITIONAL SUPPORT:

Send an email to Bill Kaufmann at Mygreenerfuture1@cox.net, along with your resume. Bill will set up a day and time to talk through your questions and respond with a critique of your resume, at no charge. Also, talk about a coaching plan for Bill to work directly with you.

Give yourself a gift of value with an email that will change your future.

INTRODUCTION:

Few people are highly satisfied with the work they do. Some are underutilized, others are not hired correctly, trained properly or supervised adequately, while others can't see their future clearly enough to understand their potential value if they were placed in the right job.

Companies large and small are looking for talented, energized, performance driven, results oriented employees at all levels. Your job is to put together a job search strategy that matches your qualities with the needs of a hiring organization. When you look at the list of requirements for posted jobs, you'll understand better the section in this handbook called, "The Purple Squirrel" from a book of that title.

When you think of all the elements that have to match between your list of "must have's" and the company's list of "must have's", you get the impression of how daunting the task may seem. Let's look at a few:

- The right level in the company (worker, supervisor, manager, director, vice-president)
- The right work experience in the right function
- The correct size of the organization in the right industry or sector
- Transferable skills that will match the needs or issues of the organization
- A style of operating or managing that matches the culture of the business
- The right time of the opening and your readiness for a change
- A location that interests you and your family (snow or sun?)
- And many more…

How to Find a Job: A Handbook of the Best Job Search Strategies For a Successful Future is designed to prepare you for the job of finding that special job: One where you can excel and prosper. The Handbook is especially written for a step-by-step progression so you can understand and follow a sequence of actions that will lead you to your goal. Scan down through the Table of Contents and you will see the extensive material to help you design your future.

This handbook gives you a clear overview of what you need to know and do. For some, it may be enough to move forward in an opportunistic way. For others who may need some hands-on coaching support, a special program has been developed to provide you with personal coaching, custom-tailored for you at a highly discounted price since you already have been through the program contained in this handbook. Contact Bill Kaufmann at mygreenerfuture@cox.net and ask for more information.

This handbook provides you not only with your Roadmap of a job search strategy, but also gives you the tools to develop a Career Map to your ultimate goal 10, 20 or more years out in time.

All this, and MUCH, MUCH MORE…

CHAPTER 1 - BE A "COMPELLING" CANDIDATE

AMERICA IS THE LAND OF OPPORTUNITY, EXCEPT FOR THE UNPREPARED

I had one of those AH-HA moments the other day that led to a question. Let me give you some precipitating facts for you to form your own question, then an answer:

- Over 18% of the workforce is under/unemployed in the U.S. (2012-13)
- More than half of U.S. employers said they were having trouble filling job openings because they couldn't find qualified workers.
- Silicon Valley & technology centers have unfilled jobs and recruit in other countries
- In the U.S., there is a major shortage of electricians, plumbers & medical technicians
- A majority of undergraduates are liberal arts recipients with many unemployed
- Advanced degrees in math & science are obtained each year by foreign-born students
- There are unfilled jobs at $80,000 a year for oilfield workers in North Dakota
- In past recessions, companies hired workers in anticipation of the upturn. Now, companies want to see the upward demand before hiring employees.
- Companies can identify their specific needs faster than people can develop their specific skills to match the job, causing a skills mismatch
- When companies know exactly what they need and when, they are looking for skills or experiences that comes the closest, and not generic knowledge that requires training
- A Master Plumber will earn four times the income of a waiter who has a history degree
- Companies are looking for applicants that can improve performance or productivity,

First, you need to figure out the issues. I see the issues as follows:

- The supply of qualified people is overabundant in some fields and undersupplied in others. The compensation in fields of demand will rise when the supply is scarce.
- Americans shy away from the hard sciences and prefer the easy courses for a degree
- The momentum of the past (have a general background and let the company give you the training) is not working. The reality is to get an earlier jump on the opportunities.
- Yes, America is the land of opportunity, but maybe less so for unprepared Americans.

The answer: Take the skills and experiences you have, target the marketplace most likely to want someone like you, then create a compelling story, resume and interview.

BE COMPELLING: HAVE A POWERFUL STORY, RESUME, AND INTERVIEW
MOVE FROM APPLICANT, TO CANDIDATE, TO FINALIST, TO NEW HIRE

There are multiple stages in a job search strategy. And within each stage there are multiple steps. We will move from step-to-step and stage-to-stage to prepare you for a new and exciting job. Our job, together, is to create a strong presence in the marketplace. I've conducted hundreds of searches and interviewed thousands of candidates for a variety of positions, in most all functions and industries... both for-profit and non-profit, including the public sector. I'll try to summarize what I've learned, what you need to understand and how to optimize your results.

Given today's job search methods, there is a void between you and the hiring manager. So...
I'll picture you as bright eyed, intelligent, articulate with light bulbs going off over your heads as
new information comes your way.

You can picture me as an older Brad Pitt with a nicely trimmed white Van Gogh. By the way,
I'm wearing a tuxedo with a red cummerbund and bow tie, plus red sneakers. Can you visual
it? You now have a mental image of Bill Kaufmann in your head.

Why did I walk you through that description? I want to make a simple point. You become the
person that others initially visualize through the words and "pictures" you provide in your
resume and telephone interviews. You become that person in their mind. You present to them
a "mental picture" of your background and results, for good or bad. So be very careful with the
picture you present. It can either enhance your chances of an interview or detract from it.

When we talk about a "compelling" picture, we mean that you stand out from all others who
may be applicants to the same job you are applying for.

THE NEXT 30 TO 120 DAYS

A job search can take from 30 days to 6 months or longer if you are in a highly competitive
function or industry, where there are many more skilled applicants than job openings. The
time-line will depend upon many factors that were outlined in the Introduction. The amount of
time you spend in preparation will determine the amount of time before a job is offered.

Usually the first 30 days is focused on developing the background understanding you'll need
along with the skills and experiences to parallel the initial stages and steps of your job search.
You will also be developing your compelling resume, marketplace approach, resource
development and support materials you'll need. This is your "getting ready" time.

In the second 30 days, you should be practicing your approach to telephone interviews,
responding to predictable questions you know you'll get given your resume. At this time you
should also be developing a Career Map, which is a flexible barometer of where you are in
your career given the ultimate goal. This is also the time you begin an initial wave of contacts
to companies and a trickle wave back of responses.

From this point on, the cycle continues at a faster pace, with more tailored resumes to more
companies while networking your resources and practicing responses to questions you know
will be asked. This is a period of heavy time and effort commitments. As you continue, you
will become more competent and comfortable in the process.

Those of you who have a full-time job while conducting a "quiet" search will spend more time
than those who can devote full time and effort to conduct an "open search. This will be
discussed later, in more detail.

CHAPTER 2 - WHY ARE YOU LOOKING?

WHICH DIRECTION IS YOUR CAREER MOVING?

When contemplating a job move, ask yourself this question: "AM I MOVING **TO** SOMETHING, **AWAY** FROM SOMETHING OR AM **I TREADING** WATER?"

Unless you know the truthful answer to that question, you may be making a terrible mistake. Understanding your motivation for a change is as important as the change itself. You want the best move for the right reason. Your longer-term career can be affected:

- **MOVING TOWARD THE FUTURE** - Will this new position move you in the right direction and at the correct level? Sometimes you need to move laterally to gain new experiences to advance further, later on. Make sure you know what you need, how much time it will take and how it will move you up the ladder. You need to look two-or-three moves out in your career in order to understand the steps you need, over time, to reach your ultimate goal. Making a major change with a shortsighted view can be a disaster.
- **RUNNING AWAY FROM THE PRESENT** – Are you looking to move to a new position to get away from your present situation? The job stress can make a change look like your only way out of a negative situation. That may be true, but not necessarily the best decision. You don't want to jump into a worse situation. Then you've got two bad moves, which means a job-hopping resume of three positions in as many years.
- **TREADING WATER** – Staying in one place for a period of time is not necessarily bad. Stability is a wonderful attribute. Just be sure the value of stability is not hiding the question of stagnation. To keep the same title and function in a multi-<u>million </u>dollar business that grows to a <u>billion </u>dollars is not stagnation: it's growth of responsibility, level and skills. On the other hand, you can't be a world-class tennis player by only hitting against the wall.

Doing the same thing year after year leaves you vulnerable when new management walks in, unless you're keeping current in your field. **There's no greater feeling of security than being in demand due to your knowledge, skills, abilities, experiences and results.** Let me put it differently: **Security is being marketable, based on your results!**

WHY ARE YOU STUCK IN YOUR CURRENT JOB?
The primary reasons people seek help finding new jobs are:
- Dissatisfaction with their current job, or unchallenging work (39%)
- Not compensated adequately to the results achieved (22%)
- Currently unemployed (22%)
- No career path or training to advance (11%)
- Lack of trust/respect with their current company (6%)

After working with <u>My Greener Future,</u> all of our current clients have either:
- Found a new and higher level job (43%)
- Been promoted to a new or expanded position within their current organization (30%)

- Currently interviewing with highly interested companies (27%)

WHAT ARE THE OVERVIEW STEPS I NEED TO ADVANCE MY CAREER?

- Assess where you are now, how you got there, and what is your next step?
- Create a Career Map to get you to your Ultimate Career Goal, over time
- Identify the leverage points to connect to an advancing position
- Research and define the marketplace opportunities
- Create a compelling resume that will provide a major competitive "edge"
- Penetrate the marketplace with high potential targets
- Develop the "mini-pitches" that influence decision-makers in your favor
- Develop and practice telephone-screening power interviews
- Practice one-on-one interviews focusing on critical issues of the hiring organization
- Understand and learn how to "'negotiate" a hiring offer
- Design an "entry strategy" for the new job, based on the key success criteria

WHEN DO YOU KNOW IT'S TIME TO LOOK FOR A NEW JOB?

First, create three separate vertical scales from 0 to 100. Designate cut points: A 50 rating is "Minimally Adequate". A 70 rating is "Acceptable". Below 50 shouts for a change and above 70 indicate progress: The higher the rating, the greater the progress.
Second, take a look at the drivers to your career success and apply them against your scale. You may have different drivers so you need to give it some thought.

When you've completed your review, add all three numbers for a **Total Satisfaction Index**. Let's take each driver separately then show you how it works.

1. **Personal and professional growth**   As an individual: Are you growing in confidence, maturity, interpersonal relationships, experience, exposure, visibility, credibility, influence, and most other personal attributes needed for the tasks ahead? As a professional: Have you increased your skills and abilities, learn higher levels of complexities, engage with higher management, expand your business and functional knowledge that continue to position you on an upward trajectory?

2. **Responsibility and compensation**   Are you increasing your functional responsibilities while expanding your compensation? Responsibilities can expand by additional roles, tasks or projects, inclusion in representative groups that will advance you within the organization? Compensation is a measure of how the organization values your contribution. It can be in performance increases above the norm, a bonus for a job well done, or promotions. Non-financial rewards are also an indicator of appreciation, like being recognized by the "big boss" in an open meeting.

3. **Freedom to perform**   How tightly are you supervised? If you've been given the freedom to develop the strategies and execute an approved plan to achieve stated results, you are where you need to be. If however, you're micro-managed or spoon-fed, it's time to ask why. Freedom to act is extremely important as it demonstrates the confidence the company has in you. Also, the higher in management you go, the greater the freedom of

action. A person cannot become an Olympic gold medal figure skater by practicing on a block of ice.

Take each career driver and rate your current position on the scale. If your **Total Satisfaction Index** is 150 or less, you have a major problem. A total number made up of all 70s or above, means you are making progress. Not only is the total number important, but so is the combination. You can be in the 90's on #1 and #2 but have no freedom of action. Determine what your best number is and in which combination. The difficultly is when all three numbers range in the 60's.

If your scores are not acceptable to you, talk with your boss if you can. Explain what you need in order to achieve your greatest performance. Your current organization knows you best and should be able to adjust easier. If not, then you'll know it's time to initially research the marketplace.

TIP-OFFS TO LOOK FOR

- You can't get excited about going to work in the mornings
- Your work station is smaller or out of the way than your peers
- Your performance is better than most but your appraisals are not
- You have periodic clash of values with upper management
- You don't get copied into communications that others receive
- You learn about a meeting to attend too late to prepare
- Important or highly visible projects get assigned to peers
- Your treated like an outsider by peers or bosses
- People avoid you at meetings when traveling as a group
- For some reason the boss is not comfortable around you, or visa-versa

CHAPTER 3 – UNDERSTANDING FOUNDATIONAL CONCEPTS

There are a number of subjects you need to understand before we get into the actual steps and actions of a job search strategy: Approaches, rationale and personal assessments.

OPEN VERSUS QUIET JOB SEARCHES - Your job search strategy is determined by how open or secret you plan to communicate. If you can't connect with great contacts because you have a quiet search, their value turns to zero.

- **COMFORT ZONE -** A fully open job search is of course easier. You can devote a wide-open communications strategy. A limited search means you must segment your communication targets to specific contacts.
- **"QUIET SEARCHES"** - You have to decide on the degree of quietness. If it's too quiet, very few people can assist your efforts. If it's too "noisy" you may find it awkward when the word gets out. This decision must be made early, before the full strategy is designed.
- **SEGMENT YOUR CONTACTS** – When you list the people and organizations to contact, you'll need to calibrate the degree of openness. Segment the list by type of communication (telephone versus email or letter), by geography (the furthest away initially), and by levels of confidentiality (who can you trust the most versus the least). Using the telephone eliminates a paper trail. No matter how quiet your search it will leak out sooner or later.
- **WHEN WORD LEAKS OUT -** You have to assume that someone in your current organization will hear about your "quiet search". The worst case is when your boss comes to you and asks, "What's going on?" Be prepared to respond to the question.
- **WHAT TO DO? -** You have to assume that sooner or later your boss will ask you about your seeking another job. You can lie (a very bad mistake) or you can try to turn it into a career discussion. It might be better to broach the subject sooner rather than later, before word gets out. In that way you are in control of the conversation.
- **HOW TO HANDLE IT -** You can talk with your boss about potential opportunities in the current organization (or lack of) versus the external world. Talk about the need for developmental responsibilities, as you would like to stay put. In other words, convert the negative into a positive if you can, by asking your boss for assistance in expanding your responsibilities or opportunities. Talk in terms of "career coaching".
- **ACTION PLAN.** See if you can get an action plan for the next 12 months. Sometimes it works, sometimes not. Be prepared for either one. Sometimes the atmosphere can turn a bit chilly. When this happens accelerate your search with wide-open communications and contacts. You probably have 6 to 9 months.

How you handle this conversation is important, for now and in the future. Handle this conversation with your boss delicately as you may want or need references in years to come. The better shape you leave a company the better your reference.

TIME AND EFFORT VERSUS JOB SEARCH RESULTS

There's a big difference between how you approach a job search and the results you get. Some strategies are time consuming but yield little in results. How do you tell the difference? Here's some insight to the value of different approaches to the market, in descending order:

#10 – Mail a generic resume and cover letter to everyone and anyone: This approach is the least effective since it's not targeted and requires the most effort and cost.

#9 – Send generic resumes to a blind newspaper ad. Ads are usually for a local position and may want your address to sell you something. They're called "blind ads" for a reason.

#8 – A compelling resume and cover letter to targeted recruiters. It's remote, but a recruiter may have a job with your requirements of specific experiences, level and price.

#7 - Resumes sent to an industry magazine ad. This usually puts you in competition, nationally within your function or industry, unless it's a regional job or niche market

#6 – Conduct an on-line national search. A large on-line website like Monster.com can give you a sense of what's available. Do a word match with your resume to the position.

#5 – Geographical, industry or functional on-line search with a targeted resume. These websites are more focused and may yield better results. Do your research.

#4 – Email lists with a targeted resume to known people and companies. After you research industries of interest, customize your resume to best fit your strengths.

#3 – Person-to-person informational meetings with past and present contacts. Few people will turn you down for a coffee, asking to learn more about their industry or company.

#2 – Network with indirect referrals from people you know. Once you network, always ask for referrals to 2 or 3 others. 20 referrals should result from 5 to 10 primary contacts.

#1 – Network directly with 100 or more of your associates, friends and others. Prioritize your list. These are your most powerful advocates who can introduce you into potential opportunities or to others. A list of 100 should eventually evolve into 400 to 500 connections.

The power of your job search strategy is directly related to the time and effort in cultivating **relationships.** A circle of supporters will follow you throughout your career for decades if properly networked, with reciprocal support.

8 POWERFUL STEPS TO MANAGE YOUR CAREER

Finding another job may be the most difficult "work" you've done in a long time. You have to design your overall strategy while focusing on tactical steps. Here are eight basic steps that we will expand in later chapters within this handbook:

1. **Understand what you want and why:** Identify what you "Must have", "Would like to have", "Want to avoid", and "What to consider" in your next job. Develop a profile. Use it against the realities of the marketplace.

2. **Develop a Career Map:** Set targets within a Career Map to show the steps along the way with 3 month, 6 month, 1-yr, 5-yr and 10-year projections. Define alternatives and supplementary activities to boost your visibility and credibility.

3. **Research:** Research industries of interest, by segments, then companies. Identify at least 100 people you know, either directly or indirectly, in priority of their potential value. Network, prioritize and connect industries to people. Start making contacts.

4. **Tell a compelling story in two ways:** Compile a list of all your major accomplishments. Write a compelling resume focused on <u>results.</u> Develop 30 second "mini-pitches" for your interviews. A mini-pitch describes the achievements that parallel the function for which you are interviewing. Focus on results, not on activities.

5. **Connect the dots:** Contact the list of 100, <u>and then their contacts</u>. It's a numbers game. The more contacts, the more exposure, the greater the potential to be "discovered". Convert the power of your compelling resume to an interview.

6. **Use a pro to give you the edge:** Sometimes a professional is your best answer to develop powerful alternatives to penetrate the marketplace. Make sure the pro is <u>full-service</u> and not just a hobby for someone.

7. **Be consistent, persistent and assertive:** Hiring managers are looking for talented "team" members. Consider alternative opportunities for part-time jobs or volunteering for non-profit organizations. Always keep positive.

8. **Close the deal:** When you get an offer you'll usually first get a phone call to make sure you are still interested and available. Try to see how firm the offer is by asking clarifying questions. Always ask for the offer in writing and always respond to the offer in writing.

Lastly, design an entry strategy into the new organization to guarantee your job success over the first year. A "coaching" organization can work with you on the best approaches.

VISIONARIES, TRANSLATORS and IMPLEMENTERS

Every organization has 3 kinds of people: <u>Visionaries</u>, <u>Translators</u>, and <u>Implementers</u>. Where they are in the organization and how they interact is critical to your job search. First, a definition:
- <u>Visionaries</u> **(V)** see over the horizon and sets the direction of the unit
- <u>Translators</u> **(T)** interpret the vision and develop strategies to accomplish objectives
- Implementers **(I)** execute the actions to achieve the results of the strategies

You need to know three things:
1. Which of the 3 is your dominant contribution? Second? Third?
2. What percent does the open job require? $V = 10\%$? $T = 30\%$? $I = 60\%$, or is the combination $V = 40\%$? $T = 40\%$? $I = 20\%$? Or what?
3. What is the dominant contribution of the hiring manager?
The answer to these questions may determine your fit for the job and with your potential boss.

What's the best combination? If your boss is a visionary, then a translator might be needed. If the boss is a translator, then an implementer could be best. There is no "one size fits all", but you may want to understand how you can best function within your work environment.

Assess your <u>current</u> organization. Who does what? Where do you fit in? How do you best function? Will your performance be affected if you report to different types of bosses? Absolutely!! If you are primarily a visionary/translator you will have a great deal of difficulty functioning in a pure implementer's role.

The most difficult jump for people to make is moving from an Implementer role to a Translator role. I'm sure you know of cases where an excellent salesperson (Implementer) who becomes a less than satisfactory sales manager (Translator). It's a question of matching and balancing these elements to achieve the objectives of the organization.

UNDERSTANDING OPERATING STYLES

Each of us has a primary operating style. The question is, "How does the mix and balance of these operating styles affect your performance?" Let's look at just three of them out of many:

The Eagle – Primarily a solo or individual-contributor role, one who acts alone

The Team player – Primarily an organizer for results through groups of people

The Stabilizer – Primarily a detail person within the group, once direction is defined

Let's take a look at them one at a time:

1. **The Eagle** usually is a sole contributor who works best on his or her own. In staff, give them a task that is not highly dependent on others' interaction, and then leave them alone to produce a result. In sales, give them an area that needs development or create new business and turn them loose with specific expectations. Be careful if you make them a manager. An eagle can work on their own <u>within a group</u> but usually not well interactively. They need to be given free rein, but within the direction and objectives of the organization.

2. **The team coach or player** interacts up/down and across organizational lines and can participate or lead groups around complex tasks. They make the best managers. They provide the interaction between functions and tasks that are critical to the performance of the business. All companies need a number of these types of employees, well placed and competent in their function. They may or may not be your star performers, however.

3. **The stabilizer** follows the work plan and is good at what they do as long as they have a manager who can communicate effectively and has high standards. Don't expect great insights or new improved processes, however. These are important contributors who usually form the backbone of the business. These are the "doers" within the organization. They get the details done while others move on to the next step.

Of course, <u>we all have attributes in all three categories,</u> but usually each individual gravitates to one or the other. So, which one are you? An organization needs all three. It's the balance of where they are that's important. Can there be combinations? Sure. As a manager, however, the decision-maker has to figure out how to put their group together so the highest level of performance is the outcome.

Why do you need to understand this insight? When you're interviewing for a new position, the group is already established and set. The question is how and where you will fit in? If you're working with a group of Eagles, the issues will be different then if they are mostly Stabilizers.

WHAT'S YOUR ORGANIZATIONAL SWEET SPOT?

A simple definition of organizational sweet spot is the kind of place you're the most comfortable and have the highest probability of success. That could mean a lot of different variables along a number of decision points. For instance:

- **Size:** Are you better suited in a large complex organization with multiple subsidiaries and divisions, or a small entrepreneurial business, or something in between?
- **Industry:** Mining is a far cry from consumer products. It's difficult to jump from one to the other if they are too far apart in their core business. Which are you more comfortable?
- **Vertical or Horizontal:** A vertical organization has many layers and the number of people reporting to a manager tends to be smaller. Horizontal organizations have fewer layers and a wider range of reporting responsibilities. Which do you best fit?
- **Product or Service:** Product-driven companies are focused on making and distributing a physical item, while a service company is focused on providing a customer value. Both are customer oriented, but the service sector is much more attuned to customer service.
- **One location, multiple or field:** Is the business in one or two locations? A field organization is usually all over the country and tends to be fragmented into smaller pieces.
- **Management style:** Are you comfortable with a strong central autocratic direction or are you highly spontaneous wanting more individual freedom in a participative environment.
- **Business cycle:** Do you thrive in turn-around organizations or do you want the security of a slow growth organization. Your performance success may depend on this dimension.
- **Domestic or International:** Global companies are different due to culture, language, laws, distribution-channels, and so on. How flexible or diverse are you?
- **Primary or secondary driver:** Is your function connected with the main business line or a side business within the main driver business? Are you more comfortable being a part of the "big dog" or rather, do you get more satisfaction growing the "little dog"?
- **And so on:** The variables are almost endless. Which variables are most important to you and how does it affect your search parameters?

Some people do better in an entrepreneurial environment while others thrive in a big bureaucratic corporation. Neither is good or bad within itself. It either fits your comfort zone or it doesn't. Which do you prefer and why? The answer will help you sort out job opportunities where you will succeed.

AN INTROSPECTIVE S.W.O.T. ANALYSIS

What is a SWOT analysis? First, the letters S.W.O.T. stand for Strengths, Weaknesses, Opportunities, and Threats, usually used in a business analysis. For our purpose, we'll look at the factors of your work experiences against the criteria for each job you are applying. It's a way to assess your attributes compared to the position description and profile the requirements the hiring organization has defined. When you make that assessment, you'll be able to understand the strategy you'll need to be successful in the interview: What to emphasize, deemphasize, substitute or steer clear.

Here are some tools you can use and approaches that may work. Look at the criteria a hiring organization has listed on their posting:

STRENGTHS – What are your most significant experiences that can be applied to this job?
WEAKNESSES – What are you missing or where are you short on experience?
OPPORTUNITIES – How can you demonstrate value or unique contributions?
THREATS – What is it in your background that might prevent you from being considered?

Now look objectively at your strengths and opportunities. Hiring managers are always looking for a candidate who has achieved results similar to what is needed in the open position. If you've done it successfully before, the chances are you can do it again.

Look at your Weaknesses and Threats. These are your "negatives". Which ones are reversible? Can a lack of skill or experience be converted into a strength or opportunity? Do you have an irreversible Weakness or Threat? Figure out how you can finesse or neutralize it. Helping a hiring manager to see greater value in you as a candidate versus your competition is always a good idea. Help them visualize solving an organizational issue through your performance.

DID YOU KNOW??   WHAT YOU DON'T KNOW CAN HURT YOU!!

- 58% of hiring companies check social networking sites to research job candidates and the number is increasing. Of those candidates researched, 33% **were not hired** based on the information found! Reformat your social networking information.
- Over 50% of communications is non-verbal experts say. But over 80% of screening interviews are <u>over the telephone!</u> We'll focus on those skills that are needed.
- 71% of candidates don't have an answer to the question "Why do you want to work here?"
- 1 in 5 job seekers find open positions from social media networks
- Only 5 out of 1000 online job applications ever make it to the hiring manager's desk
- Focusing online is only one portion of your search effort. It shouldn't be your total focus.
- Sometimes a lateral move is the key to your career success. It's one of your alternatives.
- 80% of top managers ** say that communications is one of the top skills for advancement. Only 38% of those same executives see communications above average in their company.
- You need to find out what the hiring manager's biggest problem is, and how to capitalize on it with potential solutions during an interview. Find out later how do you do that.
- For the hiring manager, hard skills are easier to assess than soft skills. Yet, the higher you move up in an organization the more important the soft skills become.
- Top management look for skills in critical thinking (73%), collaboration/team building (72%) and creativity/innovation (66%). But they rate <u>their own employees</u> at 52%, 47% and 37%.
- Do you become invisible when your organization is moving through a major transition, like a merger or reorganization? Bad move. Decision-makers may see you as irrelevant.
- A major reason why applicants are not called in for an interview is because their resumes do not convey <u>the most important elements</u> for which the hiring organization is looking.

"MUST HAVES" FOR YOUR NEXT JOB

There are two lists of "must haves". One is your list. The other is the hiring organization's list.

Your "must haves" are items that you require before you'll consider or accept another position: Title, responsibilities, location, compensation, benefits, and so on. The hiring organization's "must have" list is focused on the requirements of the position: Experiences of a candidate, comparable success other places, level of responsibility, and so on.
NOTE: It's imperative that you understand, the greater the compatibility between your list and the organization's list, the greater the probability to become a candidate to be interviewed.

One step before you even start a search or a resume is to profile what you believe is the next step for you. What would it look like when you put it on paper? Here are four basic headings:
- **Must have's** – must be a part of any job
- **Nice to have** – would be helpful or value-added
- **Avoid** – cannot be part of the job
- **Other Considerations** – things to think about

Must have: These are the things on a new job that are non-negotiable. They are givens and not compromised. Some people's "must haves" could be on other people's avoid list. For example: Relocation. The point is, these lists are to specifically tailor a search to your requirements. There is no such thing as a "generic" search. Examples could be:
- Move from Manager to Director in a similar sized company
- Increased responsibilities or new set of experiences
- Increase in compensation of at least 20% with benefits equal or better

Nice to have: These are the things that add value to the "Must have'. Sometimes you have to negotiate them in or trade off to get more "Must have". The "Nice to have" are more flexible. They offer potential and possibilities for the future, whether for future opportunities or added responsibilities. Some examples might be:
- My function would be a key to a mew business unit or at least add value to it
- Commutable distance or the company would support a relocation
- Bosses and customers see the positive value of the function rather than be dismissive

Avoid: These are the things that you cannot accept. You may accept an "Avoid" if you can neutralize it or management gives you free rein to eliminate it. People who make a change with an unresolved "Avoid" will regret it. Be very careful on this one. Some examples:
- Autocratic bosses - "Do what you're told".
- Chance of a downsize, layoff or acquisition target within 2 years
- Unrealistic expectations with an underperforming function

Other Considerations: These are the things that may not directly affect the function, but need to be considered as they affect you and your performance. Some examples might be:
- Family matters – Can you go from a small Southern town to Manhattan?
- Schools, graduation, or extended family (your mother-in-law's health)

- Travel expectations are too high at 50% and benefits are too low or costly

YOUR CANDIDACY IS DEPENDENT UPON:

1. **Research:** You must know more about the industry, company, issues, function and key components for success than any other applicant or candidate. The more you know the higher your probability of understanding how to manage your job search strategies for success. You'll then know how to write your resume and the "hot buttons" of the hiring manager. Holes in your research will produce holes in your knowledge.

2. **Compelling Resume:** As a result of your research, you'll know what the key areas to highlight when creating and tailoring your resume. The greater the parallel in content and results with what the hiring manager is looking for, the greater your chances of becoming the primary candidate. A compelling resume is your guarantee to an interview. Highlight your results not just your activities or responsibilities.

3. **Successful Interviews:** Your research and compelling resume has gotten you this far. Now your job is to "bond" with the screeners and hiring manager through a series of interviews. Focus on what you already know of their issues: Their business and functional needs, your ability to help solve their issues, and your "team" attitude. Learn how to "read" the interviewer (later in the handbook).

Your objective then, is to prepare more extensively than your peers. The advantage is the knowledge of the organization's "must have" list through your research, then blending it with your own "must have" list. You want them to want you. Your preparation and creativity in melding the two sets of "must have's" will determine the outcome of your job search

CHAPTER 4 - THINKING ABOUT YOUR OWN BUSINESS?

Before we go too much further, let's get this question out of the way. Here are some insights to take into account if you're considering starting or owning your own business.

TRAITS OF A SUCCESSFUL ENTREPRENEUR

What does the research and experience say about successful entrepreneurs? Most of these characteristics are apparent at an early age. They do not suddenly show up at age 30. Early-age traits of independence and focus:

1. **You are typically passionate about what you're doing** – You get involved, dig in, and do the best you can. You are seldom tentative or lack enthusiasm, but are selective.
2. **You tend to be achievement & goal oriented** - You continually set goals and work at it from an early age. There is a vision for the future with revisions and setting of new goals.
3. **You are usually a self-starter, persistent and accountable** - This can show up in sports, baby-sitting, paper routes, summer jobs, and so on. You don't give up easily.
4. **You are a quick learner, ambitious and drive for success** – Usually in the things that are important to you and of interest. Not so much in those things that are not. Later, as one matures:
5. **You continue to be confident, optimistic, absorb and learn from others** - You desire to optimize opportunities, willing to invest your time with things that work. You are usually open to new possibilities, if you can see the potential or end result.
6. **You know what your strengths and weaknesses are** - You learn new skills that will help you achieve success. You want to keep up with changes, like technology. You tend to be adaptable, resilient and determined, but may shy away from other things.
7. **You know your business better than anyone and a lot about your competition** – You know your business inside-out and how your own business measures up against competitors and your financial goals
8. **You can effectively manage your budgets and finances** – You know all about your loans, interest, customers and costs. You save for a rainy day, spend money to make money, and postpone personal expenditures sometimes at family expense.
9. **You are a hard worker who seldom settles for second best** – You strive for excellence, set standards, and ensure the customer is primary. You work long hours to move the business forward in the first few years, while wearing many hats
10. **You are multi-dimensional** – You are knowledgeable and can do many thing well, rather than extremely strong in only one major area, like finance (but can't sell/market)
11. **You enjoy your business but get help when necessary** - You have fun and enjoy what you do. There is a sense of satisfaction in building a future. You are not expert in everything. You contact others when warranted, delegate to staff reluctantly, as it's hard for you to do and sometimes a bit late. Moving from "doer" to manager is not easy for you.

If all of this sounds familiar, you fit the profile of an entrepreneur. The reason this may be important is if you can be an entrepreneur within a larger corporation. Then these attributes and skill sets become important for you to position yourself as a candidate, and succeed as an employee.

TO START A BUSINESS? CONSIDER THESE 12 POINTS!

This list only scratches the surface. If your not part of a corporation, you'll need a legal framework, tax advice, accounting support and a lot of hardware like office supplies, equipment, computers, programs, telephones, and so on. The 12 points are:

1. **IF YOU DON'T HAVE THE PASSION... STOP RIGHT NOW!!!** This is the #1 condition for success. If you don't have the commitment, time, effort and support, don't even start.
2. **BEFORE YOU DO ANYTHING, IS THERE A MARKET FOR YOUR BUSINESS?** Research the marketplace, competition, pricing, break-even, competencies needed and time-line for you products or services. What does the opportunities look like?
3. **OK... WHAT'S IT GOING TO COST ME TO START-UP?** Investment to start? Barriers to entry? Technology? Do it yourself or need paid staff? What's the cost to market?
4. **HOW TO BEST DESCRIBE YOUR BUSINESS TO THE OUTSIDE WORLD?** What can you do that others can't? How will you position yourself? Low cost? Quality? Service?
5. **WHAT'S THE MARKET SAY ABOUT YOUR BUSINESS?** Potential size of the market? Growth rate? Life cycle? Price elasticity? Cycle or seasonal demand? Ask customers?
6. **CHECK OUT YOUR PERSONAL PLUS' AND MINUS'** Assess your skills and abilities. Are you good in finance but not in marketing? Visa-versa? SWOT analysis?
7. **DO YOU HAVE A PLAN?** You'll need steps to consider at each stage. What information do you need? What alternatives as back up? Strategies? Time-line? Staff needed?
8. **GROW THROUGH EFFECTIVE MARKETING / EXECUTION** How to develop a positive reputation? Testimonials? Speaking engagements? Ads / articles? Customer awareness?
9. **GAIN GROWTH THROUGH E-BUSINESS / DIGITAL MARKETING** Where will the leads and traffic come from? Can you create a website? Use LinkedIn, Facebook?
10. **SO... HOW DO I PRICE MY PRODUCT TO MAKE MONEY?** Where will you position for pricing? Is there a price constraint? What's your capacity? Competitors price?
11. **WHEN TO HOLD 'EM AND WHEN TO FOLD 'EM...** What are your profit goals, by when? What is your "cash burn"? What is your STOP point? End of cash and credit lines?
12. **WHEN DO YOU GIVE UP YOUR DAY JOB?** Aggressive level?: At break-even, monthly expenses are covered + income growth of 10% per quarter. Conservatively?: All of the above plus one-year's salary in the bank! What about benefits? Retirement? Family?

This article focused on the basics of starting a business. One of the important decisions you must make is: What is your ultimate goal and how do your reach it.

CHAPTER 5 - DEVELOP YOUR RESOURCES

PREPARE YOUR RESEARCH

The more you know about a company the greater your ability to impact the outcome of an interview. Going into an interview "cold" is a mistake. Be well versed through meaningful intelligence. Do your research to excite management with your knowledge of their business. Your objective is to know more about the issues of the industry than other candidates. That's usually not hard.

RESEARCH – AREAS OF CONCENTRATION
1. **Management**– Who are the leaders and their areas of expertise? Who is in your functional area? Are they internal for 25 years or did they come from outside the company? Has there been a major change of management? Has there been an expansion or contraction of functions? Have there been reorganizations?
2. **Annual reports** – Core financial and other information. What's the theme of the last annual report? New products? Financial statements and plans? What do the numbers tell you? Employee issues or concerns? Are there issues that are concerning you? What do they say about themselves? How does it compare to what analysts say?
3. **Analysts' reports** - What does "the street" have to say? Prospects for the future? If traded, where has the stock shares been over 5 years? Upturn or downturn? What are their recommendations? Are the industry analysts in unison or divided? What are the projections for the future? Is your role important to that future?
4. **The industry** – Periodicals, articles, interviews. Is the company in the top or bottom tier within their industry? Is the industry itself old and tired or energized? Coal mining or iPod? Is the industry being flooded with foreign knock-offs? Does the company have proprietary products or are they a commodity? Where would you fit in?
5. **Competition** – Who does what better? Who is ahead or behind? What are the key differences between the top and bottom competitors? Who produces new products/services consistently? Who has the better marketing reach? Any mergers?
6. **Talk to employees** or past employees – What do they say about the company? If they could go to another organization, would they go? Why? Is there promotion from within? Are they consistent in the application of policies? How would they rate the "politics" within the company? What do they say about your function?

SOURCES OF CONTACTS: DEVELOP A DATA BASE OF AT LEAST 100 PEOPLE

What, you say??? I don't know 100 people!! Nonsense. First, make a list of all the people you know in all your walks of life going back to high school or college. Whether you worked with these people or not is immaterial. Whether you actually contact them or not isn't the point. No matter how remote, everyone goes on the list. We'll sort though the list later with a screening devise and whittle it down. Don't boot people off your list too early. You can never tell how "the network" will work. Strange things happened when you network.

Network your personal contacts – The likelihood of you being referred to an open position through those people who know you, or know of you, or have worked with you, are the highest. Why? - Because these are the people who have interfaced with you from a front row seat, or through others. They are the most credible people to assess your potential contribution. They know other people who may identify a potential job opening. So when they come across an open position from a friend or work associate, they can refer you without any hesitation. <u>These personal referrals carry the most weight.</u>

When you get 100 or more of these direct and indirect contacts working <u>their</u> network, you can add another 500 or more people on the street "representing" you. Who would on your list?
- List of 100+... family, past and present friends, bosses, peers, subordinates, neighbors going back through your relocation moves and changes of addresses
- Clubs (Rotary, golf, swim, baseball, country club), fraternities/sororities, associations.
- Service providers like doctors, lawyers, accountants and so on. The professionals, who parallel your function, also are networked into the associations and groups.
- Past vendors, suppliers and customers are a very fruitful group to tap into, as they are familiar with your industry.

Be aware, if the people who are introducing you to others are of a high caliber, no problem. If, however, others have a very low regard for their opinion, the referral will go nowhere.
No matter what the source, you need to be prepared for the questions you'll be asked well ahead of time. You need to be prepared for all situations.

SEGMENT THE LIST

Let's go back to your random and lengthy list of contacts (the list of 100+). You'll now need to find the best way to segment the lengthy list into sub-sets. The sub-sets will separate each individual into a workable category.

First, sort the list into their Potential: High, Moderate, or Low. Who are the contacts that, at first scan, show the greatest potential for assistance? Who can help you the most?

Second, sort each of the High, Moderate and Low sub-sets into categories. Categories are groups of people who have a common theme, like Family, Work associates, Direct Friends, Indirect Friends, Clubs, Social, and so on.

Third, sort each of the sub-set lists into priorities. Who within each list is the highest priority (the first to be contacted) to the lowest priority within each category?

Fourth, put the names, sub-sets and priority you just completed into a matrix with the names down the left hand column and criteria running along the top of the page, such as:
- contact directly
- contact through others
- contact by telephone - the most direct and intimate conversation
- contact by email – direct, for those you are already communicating
- contact by letter – for those who may be more formal or haven't contacted for a while
- follow-up original contact – when you contact them again for a follow-up
- comments or additional information - the place of contact and other helpful data

This matrix will give you the insights into who to contact, when, how, why, and all of the reference points you will need to develop the strategies and timing of your search, <u>by individual</u>. Your matrix will look something like this: (Use a spreadsheet)

Name/ Title	Where?	Personal?	Casual?	Letter?	Email?	Telephone?	F/U?	Comments?
John Jones, Pres.	xyz co.	X		X		X	X	Rotary
Sally Smith, Chair	Girl Scouts	X			X	X	X	Charities
Bob Hardy, Agent	Insurance		X	X		X		Customer

As you complete this matrix you will begin to see a pattern as your strategy begins to emerge. Those individuals who will be your high potential sources of contact will be first on your list, then the Moderate potential second and Low potential third. You will also see the best way to contact each person.

AVAILIABLE NON-ELECTRONIC SOURCES

Everyone knows about the typical way job seekers in the past looked for a new position: The "Help Wanted" ads. Of course you should utilize this source, but it's not be the only or the best resource. We won't spend a lot of time with this non-electronic source of information. We will add some new angles and supplements.

In addition to your local newspaper, you might want to consider to:
- Utilize your local library to expand your search in non-electronic media:
  - Add area newspapers beyond the local one, only if you can commute or move to the area the newspaper covers.
  - The regional copy of the Wall Street Journal, especially the Tuesday business section has the most extensive job listings. Consider the national edition.
  - The New York Times **Sunday edition** (or any large city major newspaper near to you like Washington, D.C., Chicago, Boston, St. Louis, Dallas, Los Angeles, Atlanta, Nashville, Miami, San Francisco or a hundred of smaller cities of interest).
  - The trade journals within your industry. These publications usually have a "Positions Available" listing within the industry or sub-industry in which you are interested.
- Contact associations in your field: Engineering, Purchasing, Human Resources, Finance, Electronics, Manufacturing, Distribution and so on. Associations usually have a local chapter in addition to Regional and National locations.
- State Agencies that support businesses looking for talent. Usually the positions are at the middle to lower end of the supervisory workforce.
- Career services of the college or university from which you graduated.
- Alumni Directory – Graduates of your college or university who are in positions of decision-making and looking for talent.

What you're looking for here is to put together an intelligence network with and for you.
ELECTRONIC SOURCES

Social network sites – Clean up and Add-value

Remember: 58% of hiring companies check social networking sites to research job candidates. Of those candidates researched, 33% **were not hired** based on the information found! That was the finding of a research report from a Social Network Survey.

Here are some actions you need to take to make your social networking sites an asset to your job search and not a liability.

First, review all of your social networking sites with the critical eye of a hiring organization. Be as objective and critical as you can. Have a disinterested friend take a look and give you his/her suggestions.

Second, neutralize anything that might diminish yourself in someone else's eyes. Take out or rewrite those items that are questionable. "Google" yourself to ensure that the web presence you have is not questionable.

Third, add into your content those elements that:
- Reinforces your primary assets or results that you are trying to communicate
- Add value to your profile that you may not have included in an application

Beyond the lists created above and the personal networking connections, the world of electronic searches is open to you. If you don't utilize these resources you are missing an excellent opportunity, especially if you are developing a "quiet" search.

Of course, the most "with it" individuals looking to connect personally and informally with those you know are Facebook, Twitter, Linkedin and other applications available to the digital media generation. These social media networks can be very powerful, but remember they are also uncontrollable. Once "out there" you have no idea where your message will go.

LINKEDIN – Used mainly for professional, it is a connector to people who are in you business network. This is a great way to maintain a link with you current and past associates.
FACEBOOK- Used mainly in the social context, it can be a great source of contacts and a "who do you know" connection.
TWITTER – Companies that have a Facebook account may have a Twitter account. It may show where Job Fairs and other interactive meetings are being held.

An important point to remember is that this is information and posting is public, so unless you have very restricted privacy settings, people can see who you are, who your friends are and what path you are following. Also, if you "Friend" or "Follow" these accounts, make sure your account is appropriate. Any pictures, comments, or information on these accounts that could be compromising should be removed or at the very least, change their privacy settings so companies cannot see this information.
Other excellent sources for electronic searches are:

- My favorite is **Indeed.com.** When you log on to this site various companies and opportunities come up for your to review. These job openings can be identified by geographic location. On the left hand side you can plug in salary, title, job type and whether it's employer or recruiter initiated. The companies that meet your criteria are then prioritized.

Many other electronic search engines are well known, like:
- Justjobs.com
- Job-search-engine.com
- Monster.com
- USA.gov
- CareerBuilders.com
- Linkup.com
- Jobslinenetwork.com
- Workfree.com
- Jobcentral.com
- and many more

You can also connect to many other search engines by using the web: **Job Search Engines.com.** Some are excellent and free, while others are web-traps wanting to sell you something. So be careful as you move through the electronic alternatives.

CHAPTER 6 - CONNECT TO THE MARKETPLACE

Go back to your Matrix of prioritized connections (group of 100). Now is the time to connect your top priority list of people with your top priority industries, sectors and companies.

- Start with the people on your list that are the highest priority, gradually expand to the moderate priority and finally the low priority. You never know where a contact will lead.
- Stay away from asking specific people for specific jobs. Ask if you can chat with them over coffee about their industry, what's going on, who is looking for talented people, what do they see as trends and do they know anything that you might pursue: Andy by the way, can you refer me to others who may expand my network of contacts?
- Even if you don't know them, there must be connectivity or you wouldn't have their names. Work the common conduits until you're both comfortable. The key question is still, "Can you tell me what going on in your industry?" Then if appropriate drill down to more specific questions. Always ask for a new connection.
- You don't need a script as you may sound scripted, but you do need a pattern or segue from when you say "hello" to when you discuss common subjects of interest. Separate out those who you may telephone from those to email or use regular mail.
- Don't expect 100% success. Some connections will go extremely well even if you didn't expect a high level of support. Other times the people who you think will be your greatest connector will fizzle out. Just be friendly with everyone, inject humor if you can (not joke telling) and continue to work down your list.
- Some people will not respond at all or won't call you back. Just move on. Sometimes an unanswered call will bounce back 2 months later with a "...I meant to get back to you but got hung up in a project. We're looking to fill a job that I think you'll be perfect for..."
- Give yourself a goal if you find the process painful, say, 10 calls a day. Then reward yourself with a good meal or time with a hobby as a reward.
- You may want to group industry calls and without giving away sensitive information, share some of the things you have learned. If other words be a conduit for information that might be of value to others. They will feel like reciprocating.

MISTAKES IN NETWORKING TO AVOID

1. Don't put yourself at a disadvantage by diminishing your accomplishments or appear to be "begging" for a job. It's demeaning and will only hurt your chances.
2. Don't' count on only one approach to the marketplace, like focusing too much time on only people you know. You must multiply your exposure by connecting with friends of friends.
3. Don't count on only one media vehicle like the Internet or social media. The greater the reach the greater the opportunity to connect in ways not possible with limited reach.
4. Don't limit your list of contacts to family, friends and recent associates. Go back to your high school days if need be, as an old friend's father may be a terrific contact.
5. Don't limit yourself to only areas of comfort. Consider moving a bit out of your comfort zone to experience a new field, or industry, or function. You may prove to be highly accomplished in a field you have not experienced yet.

USE LINKEDIN TO CONNECT

One of the best sources for connecting to open positions is through the professional people who know you. The second best sources are the people who know your people. Business people use LinkedIn to connect to others like themselves. It's a business network unlike Facebook or Twitter. LinkedIn can transform your search from a few contacts to thousands with a click of your mouse.

What can you do to utilize its power? Here are some simple guidelines:

1. **Join LinkedIn and pump up your profile:** Your profile will begin the connection. When you list your schools, prior company experience, and other basic information, you will be directed to those who have a similar background. Insert a good head shot photo to remind people what you look like. This profile will act like a resume on steroids.

2. **Connect with contacts:** This is the multiplier. The more contacts the greater the connections to others who are like you. Focus on categories of experience or interest. Lists will be provided to you, then chose those you want to connect to through a brief message. You want to set the stage for future communications.

3. **Continue to expand your network:** Tap into groups or associations that already exist for industry or functional connections. These are alumni groups, industry associations, discussion groups, and even local events that are available to you.

4. **Share information:** Share an article or post a reference to a job opening you know about, but aren't interested in. You will find others will reciprocate and a sub-network may evolve. Respond to the post of someone else's article and your views of the information.

5. **Search for open positions:** Use the segments called Job Search, Company Directory, and Job Insider among others. These sites will direct you to specific companies or opportunities of interest. They are like your personal recruiting firm directing you to job openings.

CHAPTER 7 - CREATE A CAREER MAP

SETTING GOALS

A Career Map is a series of goal-setting points of progressively advancing functions over time. It is a way to keep track as to where you are in your plan and what's next. A Career Map can also identify alternative routes and detours that may occur.

A typical road map model will look something like this:

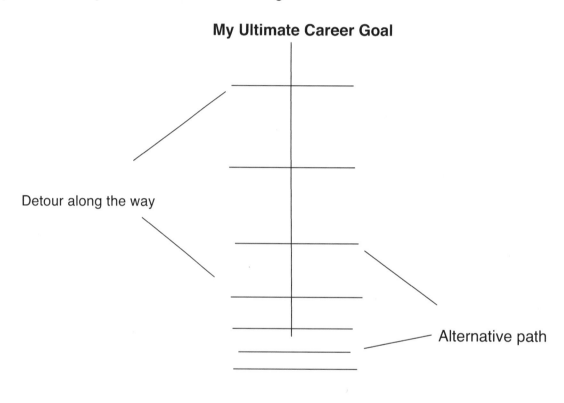

My Ultimate Career Goal

Detour along the way

Alternative path

I'm Here Now

- **First step** is to define what is your ultimate career goal when your career is in its final stages. Do you want to be the president of your own company, Executive director of a non-profit organization, Controller of a manufacturing company, a sales executive? **Define your ultimate career goal.** However, be as realistic as you can. As you move up the path of your career you'll always be modifying and adjusting.
- **Second step** is to identify where you are now. Describe where you are starting. Are you just graduating from college? Did you start your fourth year in your job? Have you completed 10 years in a function and are ready to move on? The position you have now and your current stage of life will determine a lot of the variables to success. **This is your starting point now.** Your starting point will influence the decision about your ultimate career goal. Adjust it accordingly.

- **Third step** is the tricky one. Lay out the success steps you need to make to move you toward your ultimate career goal.   This sounds difficult, and it is. What you're looking for are the known benchmarks obvious to you. Some step-stones will be <u>invisible</u> to you now, but they will emerge as time goes on. You can then adjust the Career Map to better-fit reality. Add some of the alternatives and potential detours to your map. These are the planned or unexpected turn of events. A list of possibilities is below.
- **Fourth step** is to designate the time line between each step, and the total time line to the ultimate career goal. This information will tell you if you're ahead or behind schedule. It will also give you an indicator should you modify your plan or re-designate your ultimate career goal to something more modest. The time-line is flexible because there are times when you may jump over a step, take a detour or find an alternative.

IDENTIFYING ALTERNATIVES AND DETOURS

At times an alternative route to your ultimate goal comes along that can accelerate your Career Map. Other times a detour will occur, like an advanced degree. Here are some alternatives and detours to consider:
- Do I need an advanced degree? If yes, at what stage? When? What kind? What if I already have an advanced degree but it's in the wrong area?
- What professional or industry association do I need to join?
- How long in each job position should I stay?
- Are there certifications that I must attain?
- Are there industry conferences that are of value to attend?
- What additional training will enhance your KSA's (knowledge, skills & abilities)?
- At what age should you be at each step?
- What is the ultimate time-line? Given your current age, can you still reach your end goal?
- If you don't make each step or time-line, what are your alternatives?
- If you are currently in a "detour" will it detract or help you reach your end goal?
- If you are in a detour dead end, what are your plans to bring your career back?

HOW TO DETERMINE POTENTIAL CAREER MAPS

The best approach to finding out potential career directions is to model other successful people who have achieved the level and role you aspire as your Ultimate Goal. How did they do it? Can you emulate their achievements? Do you need to adjust your plan?
- Meet with others who are in the same position you are and ask them about their plans.
- Meet with people who have already achieved the level you aspire.
- Put your goals on paper starting with where you are now and what are your next steps
- Identify the actions necessary for your next step
- Set a plan in place to achieve the results you desire

WHAT WOULD A COMPLETED CAREER MAP LOOK LIKE? (Example only) **See below….**

At age 47 minimum
At age 55 maximum

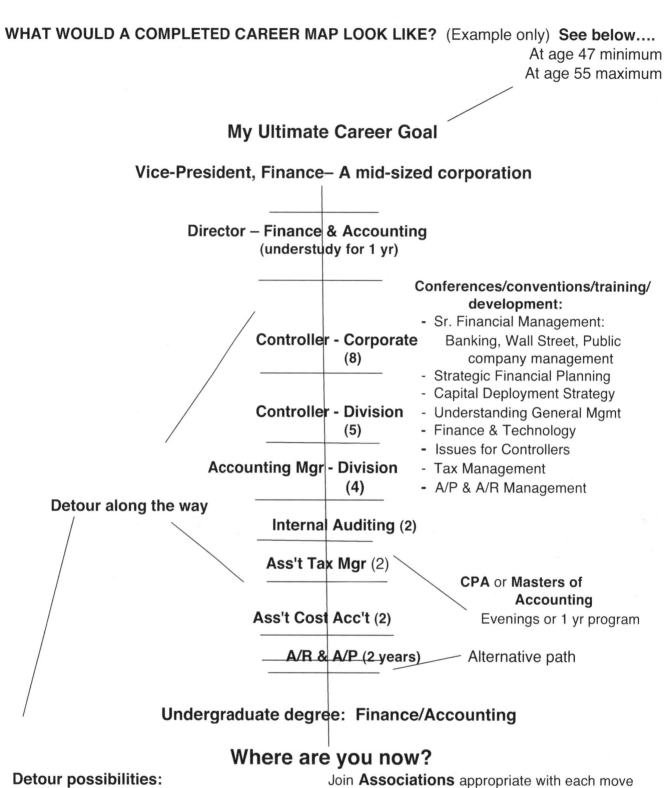

My Ultimate Career Goal

Vice-President, Finance– A mid-sized corporation

Director – Finance & Accounting
(understudy for 1 yr)

Conferences/conventions/training/
development:

Controller - Corporate
(8)

- Sr. Financial Management:
  Banking, Wall Street, Public
  company management
- Strategic Financial Planning
- Capital Deployment Strategy

Controller - Division
(5)

- Understanding General Mgmt
- Finance & Technology
- Issues for Controllers

Accounting Mgr - Division
(4)

- Tax Management
- A/P & A/R Management

Detour along the way

Internal Auditing (2)

Ass't Tax Mgr (2)

CPA or **Masters of**
Accounting
Evenings or 1 yr program

Ass't Cost Acc't (2)

A/R & A/P (2 years) —— Alternative path

Undergraduate degree: Finance/Accounting

Where are you now?

Detour possibilities:
- Corporate to Division to Corporate
- Different Divisions
- Different Industries
- Change Companies
- Different Business Cycles

Join **Associations** appropriate with each move
- Accounting
- Tax
- Auditing
- Finance

CHAPTER 8 - COVER LETTERS

THE PURPOSE OF A COVER LETTER

Your first impression with a hiring organization is your cover letter. Here are some guidelines:

- Keep your cover letter simple, direct and short
- Highlight two or three result areas that parallel the open position
- Never, ever criticize a past employer
- Hold the personal issues for the interview
- Use your own words, not those from a reference book
- Check for grammar and spelling
- Keep your focus on the open position and not irrelevant facts
- Don't brag or position yourself as a "superstar"
- Be very, very careful with humor.
- Use the cover letter as an introduction to your resume
- The cover letter is the "sizzle". The resume is the "steak".
- Limit or eliminate the word "I". Most companies want a team player.

AN EXAMPLE OF A COVER LETTER

Target the needs of the reader. Look at your cover letter from the eyes of the reader. Target the issues requiring solutions, skills that may be missing, results that are below expectations, performance that is short of the competitors, or anything else that helps with a potential solution. How do find out what the issues are? Go to the research section in the session "Preparing For The Interview" for many of the tips and sources to find out what you need to know. If you can find the key to helping any company solve an issue of concern, you will become a candidate for an interview.

An example of a cover letter is below. Please remember that each cover letter is unique, targeting different key words, roles and industries. This example cannot be used as a template for your cover letter. It is only used as an example.

June 22, xxxx

Dear Hiring Manager (or another designation, hopefully a person's name)

Your search for an **Assistant Buyer** is of interest to me.

As you will see in the attached resume, my background includes:

- Assistant to the merchandise buyer and owner of an **award winning** retail store
- 7 years experience for a **national retailer** with progressive responsibilities
- **Competencies** in sourcing, sales, stocking, visual presentation and branding

I am searching for:

- A retail position within the **Buyer** function
- A results-oriented company that supports employees to perform at their highest level

If I fit your criteria for consideration, I would appreciate the opportunity to meet with you.

Thanking you in advance, I am

XXXX XXXXXXXX

CHAPTER 9 - YOUR RESUME

THE GOAL OF A RESUME

What's the ultimate goal of a resume? Is it to document all of your achievements on a few pages for a hiring manager to review? Not really.

The ultimate goal of your resume is: <u>To create an action resulting in an interview!!</u>

So what action do you want to create?
- To have your resume so compelling that the hiring manager reaches for the telephone to contact you <u>immediately</u>, or
- The hiring manager writes a note that says, **"I <u>definitely</u> want to talk with this applicant!!"**

Then you'll get an interview as a result, which is the action you want from a resume.

HOW DOES THAT HAPPEN??

<u>The mental picture you present through your written word is the only image the manager has of you.</u> Unless you personally know the hiring manager, the only way to present yourself as a potential candidate is: **Through the power of your written words.** Assuming you meet the criteria for the job opening in the first place, your point of differentiation is how you project yourself to the hiring manager from your resume.

You need to draw the hiring manager's eye to:
- The **<u>critical words</u>** from the job description that will put you above the crowd
- The metrics or **performance results** that "jump off" the page to the hiring manager
- The experiences **<u>that fit</u>** the criteria of the position to be filled
- The **<u>actions you took</u>** that will gain attention <u>immediately</u>

You should <u>never</u> hide your results within a barrage of narrative words that overwhelm the reader.

DEFINE YOUR TARGET!!

There's great confusion as to whether to have an objective or not on your resume. Without an objective the hiring manager is looking at a generic resume. A clear, general objective and supplementary information on a resume creates an image of someone who knows what they want and understands how to get results. It's what makes you unique. How do you carry out the goal of a resume to create action?

In a succinct one-paragraph statement, define who and what you are. What are your differentiators? What can you do that most people in your profession cannot do, or you can do better? Then convert the statement to a one-sentence objective. Here's an example:

This professional has an excellent target definition **that can be converted to an objective on a resume:** "What I'm good at is reorganizing and rebuilding a program, putting the infrastructure in place, … getting the funding set up and then usually turning it over to somebody else to run for the rest of the time. I've been in non-profit management for 20 years. I enjoy the hard stuff – getting it all set up and letting somebody else run it". This statement is the core to create a compelling objective.

Here are some examples of compelling objectives:

OBJECTIVE:
- To rebuild a non-profit organization with the potential to become a premier agency
- To integrate strong marketing expertise into the business strategy of a results-oriented and team-driven company
- To contribute to the efficiency of global operations through enterprise solutions that simplify, clarify and scale
- A key marketing position with a corporation seeking higher performance and growth

Each of the objectives cited above are strong indicators of results without limiting the field of opportunity too narrowly.

WHAT DO THEY EXPECT FROM ME?

How do you answer the simple question, "What do they expect from me as an applicant?" In reality, the answer it simple. They're looking for someone who:
1. Is a Business person who understands how their function contributes to overall results
2. Is Competent in their function given today's issues and tomorrow's direction
3. Is a Compatible fit and will contribute successfully within our organization

Primarily, a hiring manager wants someone to manage business results through their function. If you, as an applicant, don't understand how you can affect the business results through your function, then a hiring company won't be interested in you. Make sure you know and can articulate what they are for you!!

Secondly, a hiring manager is looking for **competence within the function.** Do you know what you're doing? Will you support our efforts over the next 5 years, not just for today?

Thirdly, the hiring manager is **looking for fit:** Do you fit into their culture and style? How do you operate? Will you be a problem child or a leader?

STARTING THE DRAFT COPY OF YOUR RESUME

The sharper you can define your significant contributions and results the better. The closer your resume comes to meeting the needs of the hiring organization, the more successful your search will be and the easier the transition to a new position.

First, define the scope of your search through a targeted **Objective.** The Objective is a statement that overviews what you are looking for in a new position. If the Objective is too broad, it becomes generic. If it's too narrow, the fit is difficult. It needs to be strong and interesting enough to carry the reader to the next heading. The Objective leads to the next step: To "WOW" them with a summary of your results. This is where you dramatically increase their interest in you by showing them your potential.

Second, capture the essence of your potential contributions in a **Summary of Results.** This statement tells the reader why you are a strong candidate for the open position. The tailored key words parallel the open position that targets their primary requirements. The goal you want to achieve with your **Summary of Results** is to engage the reader even more deeply into the strength of your background and increase their interest in reading further into the details. An example might be:

Summary of Results: A marketing professional with a history of strong results:
- Achieved <u>business results</u> through **creative marketing**
- **Utilized customer-centric solutions** to state-of-the-art Information Technology
- Applied **financial impact** analysis to marketing results\

Notice that the **bold** and <u>underlining</u> within the text causes the reader's eye to move to those words. Those are the words you want to <u>**"jump out"**</u> at the reader:

Third, with the heading **Professional Experiences,** you now outline the actual results you have achieved at other companies. **The power in this next segment comes <u>not from the activities</u> you have accumulated, but from the power of your <u>results.</u>** The activities are almost meaningless without the outcome.

Your competitive edge: Define what you have done and can do again, not just the passive acts of the activity. Examples might be:
- "**10.1%** revenue increase in revenue through the introduction of a new product line"
- "**12.3%** decrease in cost by installing a cost avoidance program throughout the company"

Where there is a measurable result, always put it in front of the statement, in **bold.** A reader will always gravitate to viewing a number within the text. The **bold** emphasis will reinforce its importance. When scanning 50 or 100 resumes, the hiring manager will read vertically, not horizontally. Numbers in bold will jump out to the reader. You have 15 to 20 seconds to make your resume compelling.

Fourth, simplify your accomplishments from a narrative form to a bulleted form. Readers will not read word for word a hundred resumes in narrative. Wordy resumes also give off the perception that you are a wordy person unable to get to the point.

Fifth, you need to **organize** your resume to be pleasing to the eye. The resume should show continuity as you move from subject to subject. The visual appearance of the resume is very important. It may project a cluttered mind or and organized mind. You need to market yourself in the most positive light. What you are trying to achieve with all of these resume techniques, is to d**ifferentiate** yourself from everyone else. You need to stand out among your peers, and present yourself in the most favorable light.

And Lastly, when you are applying to different positions, at different levels, in different companies that are within different industries, you are best served to have different templates for resumes available to you. In this way you can tailor fit your resume to the position opening more easily. It is the same basic data, tilted to targeted skills, functions, and industry.

AN EXAMPLE OF AN UNEDITED SUBMITTED RESUME:

THOMAS GOODWILL

1234 XXXXXXXXXXXXXXXXX, XXXXXXXXXX, State
xxx-xxx-xxxx (cell) xxx-xxx-xxxx (home) xxxxxx @ xxxx . com

Professional Achievements

Fifteen Plus Years of Experience in IT and Management:

- Track record for organizing and directing groups through change and multiple business initiatives; planned and unplanned
- Seasoned manager with extensive experience in team building/motivation and delivering/writing reviews with a focus on performance
- Strong background in increasing team capabilities i.e. moving Help Desk groups to solving application issues, moving groups to 7 x 24 hour coverage, improvements in technical leadership, etc.
- Key decision maker in multiple department restructures as well as the development of comprehensive rollout approaches
- Ability to implement streamlined processes to improve efficiencies and decrease risk
- Experience in multiple business domains i.e. software, manufacturing, retail, and insurance services; experience in multiple business function areas i.e. finance, marketing, sales, customer relationships management, etc.
- Ability to stay the course on projects that require persistence and collaboration i.e. IT Governance, Change Management, data retention standards, data quality etc.
- Critical responsibilities during an aggressive implementation of an ERP system of PeopleSoft (33 modules over 2 years)
- History of continued education to keep current with leadership principles and professional development

Work Experience
XXXXXXXXXXXXXX CORPORATION   XXXXXXXXXX, State   8/XXXX to Current

Manager - IT Business Management

- Within 2 months of joining a new department and within the first year of joining a multi-billion organization was selected to manage one of the teams responsible for an enterprise rollout of Demand/Capacity Management
- Key responsibilities include adapting multiple BSA's (Business Solution Areas) to an enterprise Demand/Capacity model; as well as to identify and lift foundational capabilities as needed i.e. hard and soft booking of resources, allocation of IT demand, resource management responsibilities, etc.
- Responsible for leading a process improvement effort to expand project portfolio management to include all work consuming IT capacity such as enhancement requests, break fix, support, maintenance, etc.

Demand/Resource Manager Finance IT – XXXXXXXXX, State

- Selected to implement Demand/Resource management within Finance IT (FIT) which had limited success in implementing these disciplines previously
- Successfully completed foundational work and beyond in a short period of time to enable a

centralized view of resource allocations
- Ensured FIT Demand/Resource Management aligned with XXXXXXXXX strategic direction
- Championed relationship building between peers and other LOB's (Lines of Business) to leverage successes from all areas
- Thought leader in bringing issues to the table that would increase as XXXXXXX became more aggressive in an enterprise rollout of Demand/Resource Management

IT DEPARTMENT XXXXXXX CONSULTING   XXXX- XXXX

Manager IT Business Applications XXXXXXX XXXXXX   XXXX

- Responsible for building a support organization that supports multiple business applications as well as a financial ERP (PeopleSoft) environment
- Responsible for development of technical leads and the maturing of application processes that support critical business functions
- Resourceful in identification of members and the facilitation of groups to gather requirements and gain quick resolution for unplanned initiatives
- Critical organizer for moving back-office applications to a new data center on an aggressive schedule

Manager Business Applications Operations XXXXX XXXXX XXXX

- Improved efficiencies in applications environment; from projects to support
- Selected a structure for assessing IT processes i.e. COBIT (Control Objectives Management Guidelines) methodology
- Responsible for several groups during this time - Process, QA/Testing, and Applications
- Responsible for developing critical processes i.e. Project Management, IT Budget creation/maintenance, Business Analysis process, etc.
- Developed a plan to identify the capabilities and improve the services of the IT Quality Assurance/testing group

Manager of IT Business Analysts   XXXX-XXXX

- Liaison between XXXXXXX business areas and IT
- Collaborated with business partners to achieve business solutions through the use of and leveraging of technology
- Continued to strengthen Business Case development by actively engaging the business in writing the business case, improving templates to calculate project ROI's, etc.
- Championed the need to improve abilities to gather requirements from a business perspective as well as a technical perspective

IT DEPARTMENT OF XXX XXXXXXXXXXXX XXXXXXX   XXXX – XXXX

Manager of Internal IT Business Analysis

- Key decision maker in creating a structure that provided all aspects of support for business needs from projects implementation to technical support
- Responsible for communications and fine-tuning required as a result of major organizational changes
- Key decision maker in staff reductions due to company down sizing

Manager Business Intelligence and Change Management
- Responsible for leading staff that maintained three warehouse systems
- Championed the automation of Change Management tracking using Peregrine Help Systems
- Completed analysis and first phases of implementing Stats (PeopleSoft)

IT Computer Operations/Help Desk/Network Support
- Championed the expansion of procedures, run logs, and triggers to ensure error free operations
- Developed critical procedures such as service provider notification, global communications, and escalations procedures
- Developed Service Level Agreements with business areas and senior leadership of IT
- Disaster Recovery Leadership
- Conducted interviews to determine Application Impact Analysis priorities
- Participated in planning/ testing of critical applications/hardware infrastructures
- Developed preventative maintenance for critical Data Center infrastructures

Change Management
- Developed stake-in-the-ground processes to gain collaboration and momentum for tracking technology changes
- Developed self-serve processes for submitting, managing, reviewing technical changes

Developed Hardware Life Cycle Methodologies
- Championed the development of ideas and resources to handle IT hardware life-cycles (i.e. centralized database of technical assets such as PC's, software inventory, server inventory, etc.)
- Saved millions of dollars by implementing centralized maintenance contract management, disk management, critical procedure audits, etc.

Graduate Degree, Master of XXXXXXXXX, XXXXXXXXX University,
Bachelor Degree, xxxxxxxxxxxxxxxx, XXXXXXXXXX, State
Technical Degree, Computer Science, XXXXXXXXX, State Associations/training, Project Management, Quality, COBIT, AMA, and Toastmasters (officer)
Special Interests: CTR (Competitive Trail Riding

A short critique of this resume follows:

A SHORT CRITIQUE OF THOMAS GOODWILL'S RESUME

Given that we just reviewed the details of what goes into a powerful resume, you should add your own thoughts to this critique. Many of the errors that people make are represented in this resume. The resume is not made up. We have created an anonymous name, along with the companies and dates. But his original resume has been left unedited.

- First off, it's much too long and wordy. It needs to be edited down to one page, or at most one-and-a-half pages. Since it's so wordy it's difficult to find the major contributions.
- The reader will have an image of Thomas as someone who has trouble getting to the point. Thomas has done a lot, but the outcome of his work has no actual results defined.
- There is too much clutter at the top. A person's name, telephone number and email address is all that is required in this day of electronic communications. Putting your full address is questionable, as are multiple telephone numbers.
- There is no Objective; the reader can't be sure what the person is looking for in a position.
- Without an Objective, the reader can only surmise that it's a broadcast resume, trying to catch a job by casting out the widest net in hopes of landing something. Not very efficient.
- The Professional Achievements list is more than half of the first page saying very little. The first two words in the text is "Track record..." however, there is nothing in the entire three pages that measures results. There is no track record. It is a record of activities.
- The resume is in narrative form, which is cumbersome to read and doubtful a hiring manager will read the complete resume when screening 50 or 100 other resumes.
- Look at all of the first words in most sentences: Seasoned manager..., history of..., Championed..., Thought leader..., Critical organizer..., Liaison between..., Collaborated with..., Continued to..., Participated in... . All of these words are passive, weak or self-laudatory.
- There are six titles under one company. Thomas should compress them and say, "Progressive responsibilities leading to... ". Then list the latest and highest title and level of responsibility.
- There is no use of **bold** or <u>underlining</u> for key items that draw the reader's eye to the most important points on the resume. The reader has to search for them.
- When the reader finally absorbs the entire resume and gives it some thought, there are some very positive elements in the resume. They are hidden gems among tons of rock and are very difficult to find.

What would you add or edit in order to create a more powerful and action resume?

THE RE-WRITTEN RESUME FOLLOWS:

THOMAS GOODWILL

xxx-xxx-xxxx   **City, State**   **email address**

<u>**OBJECTIVE:**</u> As a part of the senior management team, to upgrade and update the Information Technology segment **to support the strategic direction and goals** of the business

<u>**EXECUTIVE SUMMARY**</u>: An I.T. Professional committed to the **highest standards** of performance through high quality, on time, on-budget results while **contributing to the company's success**.

<u>PROFESSIONAL EXPERIENCES:</u>

XXXXX CORPORATION – A multi-line, diverse financial/insurance company with 25 million customers
   Manager, IT Business Management   XXXX to current
- **18% process improvement** while **decreasing risk** through a <u>streamlining of operations, staff and functions</u> within this multi-billion dollar organization
- **7/24 coverage** to improve business efficiency and customer services, while balancing new initiatives to support **Demand/Capacity** and **Business Solutions projects**
- **Manage multi-business domains, while supporting multi-functions** (both line and staff) and **lines-of business,** while leveraging **Project Portfolio Management** to enhance interdepartmental effectiveness and reduce cost through process improvement

XXXXXXXXX CONSULTING– An Information Technology **consulting** company   XXXX – XXXX
Manager IT Business Applications
Manager Business Applications Operations / Manager of IT Business Analysts
- **10% reduction of time-lines** through applications efficiencies, saving millions of dollars and staff efforts, resulting in <u>more production within fewer hours</u>
- **Reorganize the Back Office** into a **new Data Center** saving multi-million dollars in time and effort within an aggressive time-line and cost constraints
- **Leveraged technology solutions** with business partners to resolve their issues, resulting in: Expanded revenue, reduced error, new business and highly satisfied customers

<u>XXXXXXXXXXXX XXXXXXXXX</u> A billion dollar Direct Sales/Retail Organization   XXXX – XXXX
Progressive responsibilities in all phases of I.T. Support leading to senior positions of:
Manager, Internal IT Business
Manager, Business Intelligence and Change Management
- **Multi-million dollar savings** by <u>resizing the structure and staff to accommodate the changing business cycle</u>, in order to meet the financial goals of the business
- **Multi-million dollar cost reduction** by centralizing maintenance contracts, disk management, procedure audits in manufacturing, warehousing, retail and field operations
- **Installed cost avoidance systems:** Change Tracking, Error-Free Procedures, Service Provider Logs, Service Level Agreements, and Global Communications Systems

<u>EDUCATION:</u>
- <u>**Masters degree**</u>: XXXXXXXXXXXXXX University, XXXXXXXXXXXXXXX, State
- <u>**Bachelors**</u> degree: Business, XXXXXXXXXXXXXX COLLEGE, XXXXXXXXXXX
- <u>**Technical**</u>, Computer Science   xxxxxxxxxxxxxxx. State

- **<u>Other</u> Certifications/Programs:** Project Management, Quality Assurance, Microsoft Suite, Cobol, TRF Analysis, Protocol Dimensions, Technology Upgrade Syste

"FUDGING" YOUR RESUME IS DANGEROUS

It's estimated that up to 35 percent that are sent to companies are not honest. It could be the wrong major in college, covering a time period of unemployment, or functions/dates of employment. Embellishing your resume is not worth it. It not only precludes you from being considered, but may also lead to your termination for cause if you are hired.

Are there degrees of stretching the truth? Yes. But the ability to check out facts on a resume for a responsible position is so easy nowadays; it's not worth the risk. Even if you are performing well in your new job, you risk dismissal not only because of the "fib", but because the company may feel it can't trust you in a sensitive position.

Use the guidelines in building your resume outlined in a prior chapter and you shouldn't have to stretch the truth. Connect key words with your results. Cite measureable outcomes. Document leadership positions. Emphasize special expertise. Show quality of achievements. Address the progression of responsibilities.

THE RESUME SCREENING PROCESS

Based on the initial scan by the manager, all resumes will be placed onto piles **A**, B, or C
- The ones that catch the reader's eye will be placed in pile **A,** for a follow-up or interview
- Resumes in Pile A will tend to be those that show results, achievement, closely parallels the open position, shows metrics, plus has a unique appeal to it
- Resumes in Pile B tend to be interesting but do not **<u>jump out</u>** at the reader. They may come close but not as close as Pile A resumes. They may be in narrative form, too wordy, and the reader does not take the time to work through it.
- Resumes in Pile C are usually not even close to a match or consideration
- Resumes in Pile C will be logged in and discarded with a note to the sender. They will never know why they were turned down.
- Resumes in Pile B will be logged in and put on hold. They are the backup resumes that are only in play if nothing comes out of the Pile A group.

Second review – This is a much more careful reading of the Pile A resumes. This is where a major cut is made.
- During the second reading, managers will be looking carefully at the detail
- This is where the names of companies, length of time on the job and responsibilities are reviewed in greater detail. The Manager will be looking at content, breadth and depth of experiences and also inconsistencies. With too many questions, they go to Pile B.
- Named companies get more attention than unknown companies (P&G will get a more

serious consideration versus Al's Deli)
- Many times the **bold** metrics and <u>accomplishments</u> (if strong enough) will get you into the smaller "A" pile group
- Once the top applicants are analyzed, all are prioritized; #1, #2, and so on

Third review - You want to be in the **top half** of pile A as one of the top 5 applicants
- Usually the best 5 applicants get a screening interview by telephone, iChat or Skype. This call will determine if a full-court press interview is warranted.
- The telephone screen is critical. It provides you with information and questions as to the issues that are to be resolved. As you will see later, the questions from the telephone screen are clues in how to interview, and what issues need attention. How to become an excellent interviewee will be covered in the Interview sessions.
- Out of the top 5, usually only the best 2 or 3 are asked for face-to-face interviews with a number of people, including the hiring manager. It could be more than 3 candidates, depending upon the quality of the individuals within the group and what the company is looking for in candidates.

Once you are set up for an interview – you become a candidate, not an applicant.

SABOTAGING YOUR OWN RESUME

There are thing you may be doing that puts your resume in the trash bin. Let's look at a few:

- Not understanding the marketplace and your niche within it
- Overvaluing your worth
- Positioning yourself as the central figure rather than the company
- Being inarticulate about what you do or what results you have achieved
- Giving unusable information because you didn't research the company well enough
- Targeting a very narrow industry segment, job function, level or compensation
- Too cute a resume that takes too much time to read
- Sending your resume to the wrong people
- A three-page resume in narrative form
- A resume that has nothing to do with the position they're trying to fill

CHAPTER 10 - TELEPHONE INTERVIEWING

"ACE" THE TELEPHONE INTERVIEW SCREEN

Your first contact from a company will probably be by telephone. Why? For the company, it's quick and easy, no schedules and no cost. For you it's a surprise when the phone rings. You may have to respond "on the fly" and the possibility to "mess up" is higher, **unless you're prepared.** There is no second chance.

Here are 5 suggestions:

1. Try to schedule a time-certain when you can call back as soon as possible. Most telephone screeners will understand if you are about to go into a meeting or are unable to talk at this time. Make sure you ask for their name, company and telephone number, even if they say they will call you. In the between time, work through and practice responses to the most likely questions.

2. Know something about the industry, sector, products, competition, and other key information. Prepare file cards for each company along with other key information. Have at least 2-targeted questions ready so the screener is impressed, like, "What are the expectations for this function in the first year?" or "What are the items in my resume that caught your interest in me?" The answers prepare you for a follow-up face-to-face interview.

3. Be aware that all of your public information is available to the screener, including Linkedin, Twitter, Facebook and so on. Know what's there before the call. "Google" yourself and change questionable information well before the call, even before applying.

4. During the telephone interview, have succinct examples that reinforce the results you have stated on your resume. Prepare responses beforehand in a crisp well thought out way. A 30 second response should: State the ISSUE to be solved, the ACTIONS you took, and the RESULTS you achieved. All questions that are asked relate to the company's needs and give you insights into your best responses.

5. Engage the interviewer in how you've resolved a similar situation to an issue. The more you know through your prior research, the better you can respond to the screener and the better able you are to connect to the job that is open. When that connection occurs, you will be asked to interview in person. Then you're a candidate not an applicant.

Lastly, be upbeat, with a positive attitude. The screener can detect an applicant that projects confidence and competence. Be that person and you will "ace" the telephone interview.

SOME TELEPHONE DO'S AND DON'TS

There is not second chance for a first impression, so plan your comments:
- Your first "hello" can put you behind. Don't be too cute, expecting a friend at the other end
- Be prepared. Have an opening 10 seconds that is positive and friendly.
- Use a land-line telephone if possible, in a quiet room without disruptions
- Keep information handy (3X5 index cards so you can carry around) with key information about the job. It's embarrassing to start talking about the wrong job to the wrong person.
- Keep the resume that the interviewer has so you know from what they are reading
- Don't try to do too many things at once, as you'll distract yourself from the call. Using the computer at the same time is a no-no as the tapping can be heard.
- Keep current on all companies in which you are interested, to either ask or respond to a question.
- Don't be aggressive on the phone. A little bit of assertiveness if OK, but interrupting a conversation or drilling home a point or presenting too strong a tone is not recommended.
- Have a list of potential questions to ask (from the 3X5 card) if at the end of the conversation the caller asks if there is anything you would like to know at this stage.
- Close out the conversation with a positive comment that let's the caller know you are very interested in the position and are excited about a potential interview.

SOME EXTRA TIPS

Some people find these extra little tips help them relax or give them an added advantage:
- **SMILE WHILE TALKING:** There are major corporations that train their customer service people to smile when talking with a customer, and even have a mirror on their wall. Believe it or not, an interviewer can "hear" your smile over the telephone lines.
- **SIP WATER FROM TIME TO TIME BUT DON'T' EAT OR CHEW GUM:** Sounds like common sense, but it works. Dry mouth can be a problem and having something in your mouth will distort your voice.
- **WALK AROUND A BIT OR STRETCH:** If the conversation goes beyond 10 or 15 minutes, that's a good sign. But keep you mind agile by changing your body position every so often.
- **PACE YOURSELF:** Many people try to get too much information out in too short a period of time. Unfortunately is can make you stumble mumble or talk too fast. It's much better to slow down and give concise, well thought out responses.
- **ANSWERS TO QUESTIONS SHOULD BE SHORT:** The norm is to try to give more information than is requested. If the interviewer wants more information they will ask.

At the end of the telephone screen interview, help yourself by following these steps:
- Reinforce your interest in the position by a positive statement
- Thank the interviewer for their time and information
- Make known your interest in a follow-up interview in person
- Send a "thank you " note if you feel it's appropriate.

CHAPTER 11 - WHAT'S A HIRING MANAGER LOOKING FOR?

AVERAGE WORKERS AREN'T ENOUGH ANYMORE

The way organizations change sometimes it's hard to keep up. The way you think about your work has to change also. Most people find it difficult to change fast enough to satisfy the needs of the organization or their boss's requirements. The boss is under pressure to change with the times too, with more pressure and demands for results than you.

In today's world, the average worker isn't good enough anymore. You need to be better than average. You can't expect to seek a promotion or receive above average pay for only average work. The same can be said for businesses that are only average in their industry. Something needs to change for that organization to survive.

The average worker is in peril because there are others who can do what they do quicker, cheaper, or better. There is only one answer. Differentiate yourself from the pack!

Take control of your career and current job and plan your own destiny.

DIFFERENTIATORS THAT SET YOU APART

Why should a hiring manager choose you? Is it your charm and wit? Nice try. Maybe it's your past experiences? Now we're getting a bit warmer, but not quite. What are the differentiators that set you apart? If you don't know, you better find out.

There is only one reason why you get hired and the others don't. You must have something that no one else has to offer. What are they? **Results!** You must have a pattern of achievements through your past experiences that demonstrate a level of results to set you apart in a way that the hiring manager can visualize higher performance to accomplish organizational objectives in the future. Let's parse the words in a way that's meaningful to you.

You have a pattern of achievements… Make a list of accomplishments that succinctly summarizes your contributions at each stage of your career and life. What have you achieved? List those things that you are most proud at each stage of your career to date.

… through your past experiences… Begin with your schooling and move forward until today, but spend the most time and emphasis on the most recent two or three jobs. Show progression of knowledge, skills and expanded responsibilities.

… that demonstrates a level of results… Focus on the outcome and less time on the activity. Anyone can implement a project, but it's the measureable results that count. Define the metrics of your performance before and after your engagement.

... to set you apart... It must be unique enough that few can match. What is significantly better because of your involvement? Separate out your individual performance first, then add in your work team, department, or company

... in a way that the hiring manager can visualize a higher level of performance... Connect your performance to the function they're looking to fill. Electrify/excite/stimulate/energize the hiring manager's view of what's possible if you're hired. You have to project your **potential** value.

... to achieve organizational objectives in the future. This is a key to crystalize your uniqueness. If you can't add value to reach their objectives, you're not going to be hired. Look both short-term and longer-term. The future is now.

What does that all mean to you? Even before the interview, identify their key issues. Develop mini-pitches around those issues. (We'll talk about mini-pitches later) Market your potential value to the hiring manager, based on the needs of the business, supported by your past achievements. Those are your differentiators. Use them well.

HOW DO I SHOW OFF MY BEST "STUFF"?

"What the heck do they want from me?" That's the question on the mind of applicants to an open job position. They want to know what the potential hiring manager is looking for in an applicant. Applicants also want to know what they need to do to demonstrate their best qualities.

There are some general guidelines that may help. During an economic stall, hiring companies want their requirements met, even though it may be for a lower level job and pay, meaning slightly overqualified applicants are applying for jobs that they might not have considered a year ago.

The supply/demand equation is currently at work, tilted against applicants. Not surprisingly, electronic resumes are receiving less attention by companies because the volume of applicants overwhelms the system. Other approaches have become more advantageous.

Let's take a look at two different views: Recruiters first, then Hiring Managers.

- **Recruiters** work for the companies, not the applicants
- They want to see applicants who consistently provide results for past employers
- Applicants who have achieved objectives beyond what was required
- People who want to learn more and strive to add value to their employer's results
- Applicants who can articulate clearly what they have accomplished, how and why
- People who can "bond" quickly and establish a positive relationship
- Applicants who show integrity and honesty in their past work history

- **Employers** want to see the "metrics" behind the "activities". Saying you implemented a cost saving plan isn't enough. Saying you "decreased cost by X% through a staged plan" is better. Saying that you, "reduced cost by X% within 15 months company-wide" is best.
- Be able to succinctly define how you accomplished your results of the past. Hiring managers are interested not only in the "what", but also the "how".
- You'll need to "fit" the culture and the organizational style to be considered a finalist candidate. Many organizations want you to meet with your potential work group, peers, internal customers and other bosses. A strong positive from them is important.

Usually an applicant is first contacted through a telephone-screening interview. The time it takes between the telephone screen and a letter of offer can be months. Companies are becoming more and more picky, because they can be very selective given the number and quality of people looking for another position. Your job is to present yourself in a way that is compelling in all aspects of your presentation: Resume, cover letter and interviews.

WHAT THE HECK IS A PURPLE SQUIRREL?

The phrase "Purple Squirrel" is a book by that name written by Michael Junge. The term refers to the "absolutely perfect" candidate for an open position, one who meets all of the exact qualifications no matter how unnecessary. Why is it called a Purple Squirrel? Because the <u>absolute perfect candidate doesn't exist!</u> Or if they exist on paper, they don't exist in real life.

Just think about all of the exact experiences, qualifications, skills, industry segment, location, education, organizational level, compensation, and anything else needed to fill an open position. What are the chances for an absolutely perfect fit? <u>None!</u> So how does that affect your job search strategy? If the purple squirrel doesn't exist, how can you be a clone of one?

Hiring companies understand that they must compromise or bend some of the unrealistic qualifications for an open position. The question is which are the rigid ones from those that are more flexible. Here are some strategies to consider:
- Form a template listing all qualifications from the position description or ad write-up
- Parallel your experiences and qualifications, shaping it around the template
- Construct a resume paralleling the template as close as possible
- Create a cover letter and include those 3 or 4 items you believe are most critical
- When you receive a screening interview phone call have all of the information handy
- Respond to the questions as best you can, focusing on the template experiences
- Make sure to ask your own "Showstopper Questions":
  - "What are the key issues within this function that need solutions?"
  - "What are the performance expectation for the new hire during the first year?"
- Answers to these questions will give you the information you'll need in a later interview
- When interviewing with the hiring manager, provide alternatives to the key issues
- Engage the hiring manager in a discussion of these alternatives

The goal is to get you as close as possible to become a candidate rather than just an applicant. While there is no such thing as a purple squirrel, you'll come as close as possible.

CHAPTER 12 - INTERVIEWING FACE-TO-FACE

UNIVERSAL Q & A's WITHIN AN INTERVIEW

There's a universal pattern to interview questions and answers. Understanding what they are and how to use them effectively can result in a more powerful outcome.

First, THE QUESTIONS: The job of the interviewer is two-fold: To extract as much key information as possible and to establish a constructive relationship. Your resume only identifies basic information. It now comes down to three **UNIVERSAL QUESTIONS**:

- **"WHAT HAVE YOU DONE?"**
- **"HOW DID YOU DO IT?"**
- **"WHAT WERE THE RESULTS?"**

The interviewer wants to find out if you are up to the task. They want to identify similar experiences that parallel the job opening. The "perfect" candidate has already done part of the job successfully somewhere else: The greater the overlap, the better your chances. When an interviewer asks a question, "Tell me about the marketing strategy you developed", they are really saying, "We have a similar situation and need someone to show us how to do it". You need to understand the question in the context of the job opening.

Second, THE ANSWERS: Your role is to relay experiences from your past in a way that intertwines with the requirements of the open position. The way you deliver that information is the key, not only in the content but also in your execution.

The **UNIVERSAL ANSWERS** should follow this pattern:

- **STATE THE ISSUE:** "The issue we were assigned to resolve was x, y, z"
- **IDENTIFY THE ACTION:** "We formed cross-functional teams, with me in the lead, and analyzed x, y, z against a, b, c, to find the critical points of differentiation"
- **DEFINE THE RESULTS:** "This resulted in 12% more revenue over 18 months..."

Since you already know the questions based on your resume, you can formulate your answers beforehand through "mini-pitches". A mini-pitch is a well-practiced response in 20 to 30 seconds to questions you know will be asked of you (more later). With this pattern of universal answers, your responses are targeted. You will demonstrate competence in your functional area of expertise. You now have an edge in the interviewing process.

ANSWERS TO TRICKY INTERVIEW QUESTONS – Part 1

Interview questions can be tricky and sometimes difficult. The simplest answer is usually the best answer. Complexity can get you into a tangle of conflicting responses. In this series, Part 1 is the easiest of tricky questions. Part 2 is the most difficult. It's assumed you have done the necessary research to understand the key elements of the company your interviewing. If not, you've already lost the interview to other candidates who have done their homework. Here are some initial questions.

- **TELL ME ABOUT YOURSELF. HOW WOULD YOU BEST DESCRIBE YOURSELF?** Provide a crisp but positive assessment, based on the interviewer. A Human Resources Manager is looking for your ability to fit in and have the basic requirements. The hiring manager is looking for specific knowledge, skills and abilities that will get the job done, given today and tomorrow's need for results. Connect your assets to the position.

- **WHAT ARE YOUR GOALS OR ASPIRATIONS? WHAT ARE YOUR CAREER OBJECTIVES?** Are your expectations realistic and can they be accommodated? Their interest is in your ability to grow with the company. Saying you want to expand your responsibilities to better support and stay ahead of the needs of the company is always a good response. In that way, everyone wins!

- **WHY DO YOU WANT TO WORK HERE? WHY DO YOU THINK YOU'RE A GOOD FIT?** First you need to understand the goals and strategies of the company. Any company wants their employees to parallel their mission. Check out the website for potential compatibilities. The question is designed to identify similar values, style and culture. You need to bring added value to performance so the business can grow.

- **DO YOU WORK BEST AS AN INDIVIDUAL OR AS A TEAM MEMBER?** Careful here! Of course you want to do both, but you can't make it sound contrived. Stating that you work best as a part of a team where you can contribute as an individual may cover the question. If you have examples of your team contributions, how you've gotten results as an individual, then as a leader of a team effort, all would be good to explain.

- **WHAT DO YOU KNOW ABOUT US? WHY DO YOU THINK YOU'LL SUCCEED HERE?** Again, your research is a must. Be specific about what you know about them: Products, growth, industry position, competition, future direction, and so on. Be more generic unless you know what the issues are and what some potential alternatives may be.

- **WHY SHOULD WE HIRE YOU OVER ALL THE OTHERS?** Hopefully you can match your impressive background with the needs of the organization. Connect new ideas and alternatives to help solve problems or add to the growth of the function/company. Never tell them you have the answers, only that you may have alternatives to a solution.

Your primary objective is to stand out as a candidate. These questions are poised to answer the ultimate question of why a company should hire you. If you are prepared, have done your research and practice your responses, you will become a candidate of choice.
Part 2 will explore even more difficult and tricky questions, so tune in next Wednesday.

ANSWERS TO TRICKY INTERVIEW QUESTONS – Part 2

Job interviews are difficult, even when you are prepared. Some candidates have difficulty with the same questions but in different settings. The following questions tend to be the trickiest. Study them and prepare alternative responses that put you in the most favorable light.

- **WHAT ARE YOUR VIEWS OR OBSERVATIONS ABOUT THIS COMPANY?** – The interviewer is looking for your insights, which could be a trap. Are you making judgments based on little or no data or solid information based on your research? Tread carefully.

- **DISCUSS YOUR PROFESSIONAL DISAPPOINTMENTS IN OTHER COMPANIES** – Be ready with a story or two around promises or expectations that didn't happen. How you handled it and what your learned. Never put down other people as the "bad guys".
- **WHAT QUALITIES DO YOU LOOK FOR IN A BOSS?** – Stay away from trite comments like, "a leader" or "likes people". Tend more toward qualities like, "To get the highest level of performance a boss needs to engage with me on strategy, then let me get the results, while being available when I need help" or a similar set of guidelines. You are describing how you work best under supervision
- **ARE YOU OPEN TO CRITICISMS? HOW DO YOU DEAL WITH IT?** – Pre-knowledge of the company's work environment would be helpful. The interviewer is looking for your attitude toward pressure and how well you respond to it. Criticism of work products is different from external competitive forces as against personal criticism. Each is handled differently: People versus things.
- **TELL ME ABOUT PROBLEMS YOU'VE ENCOUNTERED WITH SUPERVISORS**- Rather than a laundry list of traits from bad supervisors, consider examples of how a situation became your problem due to a supervisor not handling it properly. You don't want to lash out about bad bosses, but rather say, "I've been lucky to have had good bosses, but there were times when I've had to add support in a sticky situation".
- **WHY DO YOU WANT TO LEAVE YOUR COMPANY? WHY WERE YOU TERMINATED?** You need to be <u>carefully honest.</u> Never lie, but you need a credible story. You should be able to explain away most issues. Leaving a company is not a crime when well thought out and articulated. Be careful of contradictions like, "…the company is growing, but the opportunities were limited". It doesn't quite compute without a reason!

And the final curveball question that can kill an interview that has gone very well so far:
- **WHAT DO WE NEED TO KNOW THAT HASN'T BEEN ASKED? WHAT ARE WE MISSING?** A real curveball question unless you're prepared. Caught unaware, most will answer in the negative because it's almost an accusatory question like, "What haven't you told us?" However, don't be put off balance. Have a list of items already in mind. Don't' say, "Nothing, We covered everything" as you both know that isn't true. If you can cite activities that parallel the interests of the company, so much the better.

With preparation around these tricky questions you should be an outstanding candidate!

YOUR SECRET WEAPON: <u>THE "MINI-PITCH"</u>

What's a mini-pitch? A well-practiced and impressive response of 20 to 30 seconds to questions that **you know** will be asked of you in an interview. OK, let's start at the beginning. How do you know the questions that will be asked of you? Simple. Look at the ad or description of the open position on the company's website. Make a list of the "must have's" and "would like to have" that the company has defined. Then take your resume and look at it objectively.

Most questions will focus on <u>each item on your resume:</u>
- What did you do?
- How did you do it?
- What was the outcome?

Here's an example to the question: **"HOW DID YOU OBTAIN THOSE RESULTS?"** (You're interviewing for a Marketing Analyst position in a consumer products company, talking about an item on your resume). Your <u>mini-pitch response</u> would be something like this sequence:

Issue: "Our revenues had been flat for the past 2 years".
Action: "We researched our customer's buying patterns by analyzing consumer behavior models. After comparing the development costs for a new product versus re-branding an older product, we introduced a new line to a new market".
Results: "The outcome was a 12.2% increase in new orders from new customers over an 18 month period".

This is **a 61-word mini-pitch in 21 seconds.** You practiced the answer because you knew the question that was most likely to be asked. When you answer, you will sound confident and competent. You've made a positive impression with the hiring manager because you provided a full response without a distracting narrative of irrelevant details.

Listen very carefully to the hiring manager's follow-up questions. They will give you critical insights into the real issues within the organization. Once you understand the hiring manager's direction, you can guide the discussion to your advantage.

Mini-pitches are essential to understand, create and practice. It separates you from other applicants who may not be as prepared as you. Mini-pitches also force you to target answers in a way that demonstrates your ability to focus on the things that are important. From the hiring manager's perspective you show the ability to "think on your feet" in an articulate way.

LEVERAGE THE MINI-PITCH TO A HIGHER LEVEL WITH THE HIRING MANAGER

Now is the time to convert your effective mini-pitches into an engaging discussion with the hiring manager. This conversion happens by shifting the emphasis from your positive results of the past, to potential successful strategies for the future. The transition is accomplished by focusing on alternative solutions of issues within the open position for which you are interviewing. Whoever can engage the hiring manager in discussing potential solutions to the issues of the organization, with alternatives and/or potential strategies, will usually win the job.

How do you accomplish that transition? Connect the results and solutions you have experienced in similar past situations to the issues facing the hiring manager. For example:
- During the interview, as you respond to questions using mini-pitches (the issue, the action, the results), the hiring manager will ask follow-up questions like, "How did customers respond?" or "How long before results were achieved?" or "How did you get senior management buy-in?" Whatever the question, it gives you insight into <u>the real issues</u> of the hiring manager. No question is irrelevant! Any and all questions will be directly related to what the hiring manager is looking for in the "ideal" candidate. You just have to listen.

- Respond to the follow-up questions by describing the steps you went through that may be helpful to the hiring manager. The "interview" will now evolve into a "discussion" of potential strategies. Possible discussion items may include:
    - Alternatives that were considered
    - The pro's and con's of each alternative
    - The implications if implemented
    - The resources required and the cost/benefit analysis
- Tighten up the discussion of strategies that may provide solutions to specific issues of the hiring manager. You might want to say, "A number of these alternatives may be applied to your situation. Would it be helpful for me to give you more details to those issues you find particularly attractive?" If the answer is "yes", you know you have made an impression. Now is the time to shine. Your supportive candidacy will rise to the top.

The reason a mini-pitch takes between 20 and 30 seconds is to allow time enough for the follow-up questions from the hiring manager. If you assume your interview as a candidate will take about an hour or so, you need to make sure you have enough time at the end of the interview to begin the discussion about strategies to potentially resolve current issues.

An objective of the interview is to guide the discussion to your advantage. Your task is to link your answers to the hiring manager's issues, so you are perceived as part of the solution.

THE "SHOW STOPPER" QUESTIONS

Interviews are a curious way to find a job. It's kind of like going on a date: Everyone is dressed up, on his or her best behavior, and move through a choreography like in a written script. Now ask yourself, "How can I differentiate myself from all others so I'm the candidate of choice?"

There are basically three different kinds of interviews: First, the telephone interview to check you out. Secondly, as a result, there's a screening interview. Third, you interview with the hiring manager. Within each interview there are 3 segments:
1. To start off they'll say, "Let me tell you a little bit about the company"
2. Then they'll get to the heart of what they want, by saying, "Let me ask you questions about your background and experiences"
3. Lastly they casually ask, "Do you have any questions of me?"

It's during this last segment "Do you have any questions for me?" where can make a significant impression with your **Show Stopper** questions. Your objective during an interview is to answer all the questions intelligently, but you also need to **ask** the right questions. These questions, from you to the interviewer, will separate you from other candidates. The answers you receive from the **Show Stopper** questions will provide you with the information you need to design and excel at the next round of interviews.

These questions will also impress the interviewer that you are a businessperson in addition to being a qualified candidate for the open position.

What are the **Show Stopper** questions? First, during the telephone-screening interview you need to ask these key questions: <u>**"What are the key issues in this function that need to be solved?"**</u> and second, <u>**"What are the performance expectations for the new hire during the first year?"**</u>

When you extract that information during the telephone interview you will be prepared for the next phase of face-to-face interviews, as you now know what they are looking for. Your responses can now be customized to fit the "key issues" and "performance expectations" that you extracted from the telephone interview.

During the interview with the **hiring manager,** your objective is to <u>engage</u> in a discussion around actual issues that are important: Issue definition and potential alternatives for solutions. Since you already know the key issues and performance expectations, two items are key to your success:

- Shape your answers to the questions based on your prior interviews that will help solve the hiring manager's issues. Lay out alternatives, pro's/con's and implications that can lead to potential solutions.
- Develop an interactive relationship with the hiring manager. The mental question of the hiring manager will be: "What can this candidate bring to my organization that will add value to my results?" Your job is to answer that question without it being asked. **Show Stopper** questions are the key.

When the hiring manager sees you as a problem-solver to the issues that need resolution, you become a <u>primary </u>candidate. Now it's just a question of "closing the deal".

"READING" YOUR INTERVIEWER

All interviewers have a primary style or approach. If you can determine their style, you can influence the outcome. All you require are some telltale signs for the best approach. It's relatively simple, but very powerful when done well. Here are some insights:

Interviewer's characteristic style:

- <u>**Results/Action Style**</u> – Questions come quickly and are targeted. Impatient. <u>Assertive,</u>
    - Quick, short questions on accomplishments, achievements and future contribution
    - Little time for chitchat. Drive to the core questions. Take charge immediately.
  Response: Answers should be short, accentuating the outcomes of past actions, but be ready for the "how did you do that?" question. State the **issue, action, and results.**

- <u>**Thoughtful/reflective Style**</u> – Wants facts, analysis, numbers "talk", measurements, ratios
    - Focus is on "their" area of responsibility, "issues that affects me or my group"
    - Typically are more comfortable with numbers, not personal or social relationships
  Response: Answers can be more expansive, but relate to the rationale behind the decision. Why one option over another? Focus on how you measured results?

- **Relationship-oriented Style** – Interactions, group emphasis, compatibility, team orientation
    - Focus is "fitting in", part of the support network. A productive part of the "team"
    - Will put you at ease to increase your comfort zone and theirs. Positive relationships.

  Response: Emphasize the "we" not the "I". Look for common values and consensus views. Involvement and inclusion is important even though the decision is theirs.

- **Get-along Style** – Provides support but doesn't lead, avoids controversy, seeks balance
    - Focus on the neutral, "no big changes to upset my world". A rebel is to be avoided.
    - Stability is important, status quo, change should come in small doses

  Response: Reinforce the positive results of the past, the need to add value, but on a planned incremental strategy. Seek their ideas and positively reinforce past outcomes.

What to look for to determine which style is prominent:
- **Their offices and external signs:**
    - Strong action-oriented: Spartan. Functional. Few personal items or nick-knacks.
    - Thoughtful/reflective: College degree on the wall. Reports or papers piled high.
    - Relationship oriented: Personal pictures, boat/hobby. Chairs grouped around a table.
    - Get-along: Pictures of family/dog, a bucolic sunset. Neutral office in color and décor.
- **Their behaviors:**
    - Strong action-oriented: Few social niceties. Intensity. Short meeting. Looks at watch.
    - Thoughtful/reflective: Overanalyze details. Thinks about alternatives/implications.
    - Relationship oriented: May talk about themselves. Longer meeting. More casual.
    - Get-along: More passive. Least formal. Looks for connections. Seeks your view first.

Of course, there are always exceptions to the rule. The higher the level of manager the more difficult it may be to assess a style. If you're in a conference room there are far fewer clues to "read". Good luck.

NON-VERBAL CONNECTIONS WITH THE INTERVIEWER

Here are a couple of non-verbal considerations to make your interview more positive:

- **Smile from time to time, especially when the interviewer says something you agree.** Someone who is somber is less likely to make a positive impression.
- **Make eye-to-eye contact.** Looking all over the place, or worst, looking at your feet is not only uninspiring but also rude. It's a turn-off for the interviewer who isn't sure you're even interested. Your want to establish rapport especially when listening.
- **Sit up straight in an interested position.** When you lean forward it signals a higher level of interest. When you lean back is a sign of lesser interest. When you're talking, do the same and you will tend to draw the interviewer into what your saying.
- **When the interviewer says something interesting or you agree with, simply nod your head.** This is a subtle cue that you and the interviewer see things the same. It also demonstrates that you are listening carefully to every word.
- **Physical distance.** Americans are comfortable within an arms length, the English about one-and-a-half arms length, Mid-Ease much closer. Be aware of their comfort zone.

DIFFERENT KINDS OF INTERVIEWER THAT ARE UNUSUAL

You will experience different kinds of interviewers as in life. How you manage the interaction is important. Some interviewers will start out very passive and gain energy as the interview moves on. This is usually a sign they are warming up to you. Here are some added thoughts:

- **The less experienced interviewer** – This person could be new to the interviewing experience or unprepared. Give them a nudge like "What would be of value for you to know about me or my background?" This usually will jump start their taking more control.
- **The Sphinx** – This is usually a shy person or someone not comfortable in the interviewer position. Try to engage them in a subject that they are comfortable like their job or about the company itself. One wonders why you are interviewing with this person if you are a truly potential candidate. If this is your potential boss, steer clear.
- **The "know-it-all"** – Many times the dominant interviewer who can't seem to stop talking is nervous or uncomfortable with the interview. It could be that you intimidate them. See if you can turn the conversation around to "work-with" or support efforts or teamwork.
- **The rambling interviewer.** There seems to be no continuity or flow of the interview. Sometimes the questions are not related to the job. Your effort should be on bringing the conversation back to the open position. Ask, "How is that relevant to the open position?"
- **The "dentist" interviewer** – This is the person who hammers away at questions like a machine gun. It's hard to keep up, but try to respond in a meaningful way. This is where the mini-pitches come into play. This is usually the intense driven interviewer.
- **The predictable interviewer** – Usually this is the easiest to interview as you can almost predict the questions and direction of the interview. Keep them in their comfort zone. They are usually open to questions from you, indicating your interest in the position.

CAUSING SELF-INFLICTED WOUNDS IN AN INTERVIEW

Some of these mistakes are deadly. Others will diminish your candidacy, so be prepared.
- **Buzz words with no "back-up":** When a statement is made that can't be proven
  - Ever see a resume that said, "Non-creative individual with no goals or results, with a total lack of motivation, looking for a high paying job while doing little"?
  - How about, "Innovative worker, achieves objectives, highly motivated, looking for high reward with high performance"?
- **What's in it for me?** – The self-absorbed applicant looking out for number 1
- **Complaining** – Will define how the world has been against them
- **Looking for another job:** All their fault, I'm a victim, politics, boss won't let me
- **I deserve it... :** A feeling of entitlement or attitude that wears thin quickly
- **I don't take responsibility... :** It's someone else's fault or I'll never say I was wrong
- **My background is the Great American story:** I lead a charmed life

It's interesting to note that the people who get the job may be seen by others as being "Lucky", but tend to be more relaxed, confident in their abilities and have a positive attitude.

CHAPTER 13 - AFTER THE INTERVIEW

TAKING NOTES RIGHT AFTER YOUR INTERVIEW(S)

It's critical that you write down important notes as soon after the interview as possible. If you meet with multiple people, see if you can take a breather between meetings and jot down notes for each meeting. Your mind is sharpest and your memory is at its height immediately after each meeting. These notes can make the difference between understanding the critical issues and having them fall through the cracks because they got lost in the mix.

The reason why note taking is important centers on a number of important considerations:
*   What is new information that you don't want to forget? What did you learn?
*   Information about the company, the function or the job that is different from your perception
*   Profile insights about people you just interviewed or those that you hope to interview
*   Insights about the direction, issues, concerns, strategies, short-falls or competitors
*   Anything that is worthy of noting. Items for you to give more thought and consideration.

You may find that events or discussion points which did not make sense at the time, will become clearer later on. These points may fit a pattern not seen during the interview but will become obvious to you upon reflection. Of special note are the questions that were asked by the interviewer that were out of the context of your expectations.

You are looking for tidbits of information to make your next interview more substantial, especially if it's with the hiring manager. Any intelligence you can accumulate from individuals already in the company will position you that much further toward the finalist category.

YOUR FOLLOW-UP COMMUNICATIONS

If you're interviewing for a part-time position at the local pizza place, you may not need a follow-up, hand written note to your potential employer. Depending upon with whom you interview, at what level and under what circumstances, different methods of correspondence are suggested:
*   **For lower level positions** in a more casual organization, an email "thank you" note may be acceptable, especially if you know the person. If you don't know the manager, then a higher level of communications would be advisable.
*   **For a supervisory/managerial position** it necessitates a written response that emphasizes your ability to communicate effectively in writing. A personal hand-written note indicates a strong interest in the position.
*   **The higher the level and status** of the individual you are writing to, the better quality of paper and envelope. The letter may be on bond paper or embossed stationery. This would be especially true if you are communicating to an officer of a company. A professional recruiter would also be in this category.

The content of the communications should match the level of interest and relationship you believe exists between you and the recipient of the letter:
- If you sense a strong positive bond was established, then try to capture that in the letter
- If the meeting was more formal, then reflect that tone

Don't try to make the relationship something that it's not. Humor is an extremely difficult thing to do, so don't take the risk of a misunderstanding. Communications is an art form, so don't try to "rig the letter" to be something or someone your not. Experts in communications will tell you that:

CONTENT OF A FOLLOW-UP LETTER

Hopefully, right after the interview you took notes of the important elements of the meeting. Why? Because your notes should hold important clues to the needs and requirements of the organization for the position you just interviewed. Some of that information might be helpful in a follow-up letter.

The follow-up letter should, of course, thank the interviewer or manager for their time and helpfulness. Refer to whatever came out of the interview that leveraged your insight and increased your comprehension of the needs and requirements of the open position. The following example of a "Thank You" letter does a number of things:
First, put the emphasis on the hiring manager's goals. Make the hiring manager aware that you know what's important
Second, use the words from the ad and of the hiring manager to define the responsibilities. It demonstrates that you listened well, and understands the issues.
Third, connect your knowledge and abilities to finding solutions to the needs of the business.
Forth, identify that you are genuinely interested in pursuing this position.

End the note on a point that you would like to move forward with another, more detailed meeting.

COMPARING COMPANIES WITH EACH OTHER

When you have more than one company, take your Matrix list of "Must have's" against the companies you want to compare. Rate each attribute against reality as you view it. Evaluate each criterion against your standard. You can use a value scale from 0 to10, with 10 as the highest, and 5 being minimally acceptable. **Do your own. (Don't use the example)**

However, remember that interviewing is a lot like dating. Everyone gets dressed up and is on their best behavior, with all of the social niceties. Situations and personalities are different as the situation changes and the business cycle shifts from positive to negative to positive.

Some people thrive during those times of adversity while others wilt.   See the example below.

DECISION MATRIX – CRITERIA FOR ASSESSING KEY FACTORS
(Scale of 0 to 10 with 5 minimally acceptable)

MUST HAVE's

	Potential Job #1	Potential Job #2	Potential Job #3
- Fits into my long range career goals	8	7	5
- Increased responsibilities or new set of experiencs	7	6	6
- Increase in compensation or potential for greater income	8	8	9
- Comfortable fit with management philosophy	6	6	6
- Positive & supportive boss	7	7	5
- Promotion possibilities	7	6	8
- Ability to use my skills & provide needed expertise	8	7	8
- Benefits are equal or better than current	7	7	6
- (list personal issues)			
- schools			
- relocation			
- and so on			
TOTAL	58	54	53

NICE TO HAVE

	Job #1	Job #2	Job #3
- My function would be a key to the future success	7	7	7
- Commutable distance or company support relocation	6	6	6
- Strong, supportive & competent subordinates	5	6	6
- Peers see the value of the function	6	6	6
- Potential customers are looking for help	5	5	5
- and so on			
TOTAL	29	30	30
GRAND TOTAL	87	84	83

AVOID (LOW IS GOOD)

	Job #1	Job #2	Job #3
- Autocratic bosses - "Do what your told"	L	L	M
- Chance of layoff/downsize/acquired within 2 years	L	M	H
- Lack of top management support to the function	L	L	M
- Unrealistic expectations	L	L	M
- Other...			

WHEN ASKED FOR REFERENCES

Providing references can be tricky. Figure out the best of who and when.

References can be either professional or personal. Professional references are related to your work experiences and past employers. They usually come from bosses or a higher authority within the work environment. The higher the level, the higher the value that other ascribe to it. A reference from a president is usually "worth more" than a reference from a manager in the same organization.

Always ask an individual first, if he/she is willing to provide a reference. Do not put a referenced person in the awkward position of a surprise telephone call from a potential employer about you, without their knowledge.

Personal references are only used or useful if you have no professional references. Personal references are not work related and have little value to a potential employer. All a personal reference can say in so many words is, "This is a nice person".

Depending upon whether your search is open or quiet may determine the timing of providing a list of references. If it's an open search that everyone knows about, then references can be provided at almost any time. Just be careful that multiple companies aren't contacting your references at the same time. It could prove confusing and awkward.

If you are conducting a quiet search, however, wait until the last minute to provide references, for obvious reasons. References can provide substance to your past experiences, but not much more, unless the hiring manager knows of the person doing the reference and trusts the judgments that are made in the reference.

One other consideration: Some employers will contact the prior company to check out your documented compensation, hire and separation date and any other information they can get. So don't fabricate information. While your personnel file is confidential, the information within it can sometimes be compromised. Surprisingly enough, some companies will Google your name on the web or go into Facebook to see what's there. Be forewarned.

CHAPTER 14 – NEGOTIATING AN OFFER

WHEN YOU GET AN OFFER

Let's assume everything works out well. The hiring company wants you and you want the job. Now what? You get a telephone call offering you the position. What do you do?

Tips on negotiating

Usually an employer will outline the conditions of the employment offer. Make sure it coincides with your understanding of the position. Some of the basics are the title of the position, compensation, incentive bonus if applicable, reporting relationship, outline of duties, starting date, and the start of various benefits (as some have a waiting period).

After you hear and understand the basic elements of the offer, be polite (even though the offer may be less than you anticipated) and say, "Thank you very much for the opportunity. I'd like to give it some thought, talk with my spouse, and get back to you. May I call you with questions we may have?" The company spokesperson will always say "yes, please call me with any questions you may have about the position or the offer". They will of course ask you how much time you'll need, so be prepared for the question. They may have a back-up candidate waiting in the wings, so don't take too much time.

Your objective here is to see if you can differentiate between "hard core' policies/practices and those that are more flexible within the offer. If you can, find out how the policies/practices differ by various levels of management. Usually supervisors are treated differently than vice presidents in terms of the flexibility within the policy and exceptions to it. What are the negotiable items? What typically are not negotiable? Are there trade-offs that can be discussed? If the salary is less than you anticipated, can there be a 6-month review and a potential increase at that time? Instead of the usual moving policy, can you suggest a more tailored approach?

Usually those items that involve third parties (insurances, pensions, 401K's and the like) are not negotiable: They are fixed by the policy, contract or law. Anything else that is within the company's decision is negotiable. The only caveat is the greater the request that is out-of-policy, the higher in the organization the decision has to be made. The Human Resources Department can make some decisions, others by the Department Head, while some may need an officer and a few exceptions only the President can determine. Experience tells us that the level of flexibility is directly related to how motivated the company wants to hire you. If they see you as a commodity, your negotiating level is very low. If you are seen as the answer to their problem, you have a great deal of flexibility.

HOW TO APPROACH COMPENSATION

Compensation is always tricky on both sides. From the company's perspective it's difficult to pay you more than someone internally, who has been with the company for 10 years and is in a peer function. There are also compensation ranges and comparatives within the industry that may be at play.

From your perspective, you want to optimize your going-in compensation because it's easier to negotiate a compensation package now, versus once you're in the company. Offers can be a low-ball test to see if they can get you less expensively, but that's not always the case. You might ask the question, "Is that your best offer for compensation, as I was looking for $xxxxxx, instead of $xxxxx". Usually the response will either be, "The salary is set and there is no room to increase it at this time", or "There may be some flexibility that we can talk about".

You need to determine what is important to you. Do not accept an offer that you feel is beneath your value, as your resentment will linger. Are there ways, over time, to accelerate the compensation through performance, incentives or promotion?

One of the things that could be helpful to you is a comparative analysis of this position to the marketplace. There are industry studies, functional reports, area comparisons that are available in your local library, or on-line (usually for a fee) or network with others who may know more about it than you. It would be fruitless to challenge the data source of the company, but anecdotal information is helpful.

Keep the communications open and positive. Never let the conversation devolve into an ego or personal discussion, even though the outcome is very personal. Remain professional and reasonable when discussing a "come-back" proposal or "trade-off".

Whatever the outcome... **Always get the final offer in writing. Give your acceptance in writing.** And by the way, send your acceptance by registered mail, receipt requested or FedEx. There are stories of candidates getting verbal offers that somehow fall through. You never want to resign from your current position until you are fully committed to the transition to a new organization and they are fully committed to you. If you are the least bit concerned about an offer, seek a contract attorney's opinion. Offers of compensation are usually stated in terms of the usual pay period, not annualized. That's because an annual number has been certified in some courts as an annual contract.

WHY DO OTHERS GET THE JOB OFFERS AND NOT ME?

Most candidates never know why they weren't selected for a job they really wanted. It's frustrating to always come in second place. Here are some of the reasons.

Take your pick:

- **Internal candidate** – There is an internal candidate in place, but they wanted to "test the external marketplace" to see what else is out there. The chances are slim for you.

- **The "specs" are against you** – Sometimes the company is looking for a specific candidate because of different mandates. They may need a female or minority or any number of categories of which you are not one.

- **Human Resources selections** – Many times the HR people get to narrow down the selection before the hiring manager gets to interview.

- **Your resume versus the computer** – In larger companies the computer looks for key words to match against the flood of resumes. If your words don't match, you're out.

- **You don't fit our profile** – For some reason the decision is made that you don't fit into the culture of the organization. This will happen most frequently with a group interview.

- **Over or under qualified -** Your background and experiences either fall short or are over the top for what they are looking for in a candidate.

- **The company wanted to see who is out there** – The company puts out an ad for a position that may not exist just to see if competitor's key people respond.

WHAT CAN YOU DO ABOUT IT?

Be as targeted as you can, persistent and prepared with the skills you need. Cross-reference your strategy with those that seem to work for others. While all are important it's the integrated "package" that's important. Check them out.

- **Your background, knowledge, skills, ability and experience** – Companies look for the best match possible. They want someone who comes closest to having experienced the results they want. They're not looking to train a "newbie

- **You have demonstrable results** – Listing your activities won't cut it. Unless your can quantify or qualify the measured results you've achieved, you can't document your success.

- **A compelling cover letter and resume** – A cover letter should be strong enough that the reader is highly motivated to read your resume. The first step is the resume that leads to the hiring manager to take the next step, an interview.

- **Continuity, progression and flexibility** – Employers always look for candidates that don't jump to new companies each year. They like to see positive movement up the responsibility ladder rather than someone doing the same thing year after year.

- **Your projected persona** – How do you project yourself and your results? Your interaction with the hiring manager is critical.

- **You're able to relate to almost anyone** – Employers are looking for "team" members who can play well with others, not someone who will cause conflict.

- **Your attitude, passion and energy**- Do you affect people in a positive or negative way? Complainers are usually avoided, especially when talking about current bosses.

- **Your ability to put it all together** – Putting a full package together for a job search strategy is critical to achieving success. Having only one or two elements aren't enough.

Experience shows:
- You need a dynamic job search strategy in order to accelerate your career
- You may be missing a few key skills necessary to become a finalist candidate
- You need to differentiate yourself above all others within the marketplace
- Your key results need to be designed to align with the needs of the hiring organization
- Your potential contribution has to solve today's issues and tomorrow's needs

These strategies and skills can be learned within a short period of time. Miss one of these items and you may come in second best.

HOW TO QUIT IN A POSITIVE WAY

How you quit your job may have a lasting effect on your career. Do it correctly and you have a lasting legacy. Do it incorrectly and you'll have a difficult time changing the effects.

The key is to never quit angry. Always try to quit in a positive way, even though you'd like to make all of your thoughts known to anyone that would listen. Even though you hate your current job, make your exit in a dignified yet neutral way. It isn't productive for you or the organization to make a list of all the thing wrong with the boss or company. Be careful that your negativism doesn't transfer over to your new job. Step over the impulse to lash out and never look behind.

Your resignation letter should be short and sweet. Don't look for revenge or "payback". Simply state your termination date giving the organization appropriate time. The higher you are in an organization, usually the more time you give. Sometimes an organization will want you gone before the date you give, however you are still due your salary, benefits and vacation time accrued.

Be extra careful to overlap or integrate your benefits, especially health and life policies between the old and new companies. You don't want an exposure time that will make you and your family vulnerable if something happens.

EXIT INTERVIEWS

From the company's perspective, an exit interview can be a valuable tool to identify potential issues that need to be resolved. However, the potential for the information to leak into the organization in a way that may not be helpful to you, is great.

If your current organization is fixated on an exit interview and you feel responsible to follow their policy, you have an alternative option. Ask for the questions in writing and you will respond in writing, dated and signed by you. If you have a major concern as to what goes in your personnel file, ask for a copy, as is your right. In that way you can see what is there and have a document that can't be changed.

Sorry to be so negative about this subject, but I have seen too much over the years where the individual wrongly targeted without their knowledge.

CHAPTER 15 - ENTRY STRATEGY

When entering a new organization, think carefully about your first 90 days. This time frame can make an enormous difference at to how you are perceived in the organization. Consider:

- **Do a Needs Analysis within the first 30 days** – define what you have, why, what might be done differently, what are the critical issues short term, immediate action, what is critical. The higher in an organization you become, the greater the need for an audit or "base-line" of your taking over. Why? Because the longer you are in the job, the greater the assumption that you "own the past". If there was anything hidden from you that you don't know about of a legal or malfeasance point of view, it's yours, unless you show that you took the effort to identify major issues. Without a "due diligence", not matter how complete, at least you have shown a fundamental attempt to define what it looked like when you came into the position. It's also a base line that you can show over time the performance strides since you took over. Without it, you have little measurement criteria to show your results.

- **Share the results with your boss within 60 days** – With your boss, prioritize and lay out an action plan, sequence of strategies, projected outcomes, issues needing resolution, and so on.

- **Final 30 days begin the implementation** – Maintain weekly updates with your boss, lay out alternatives and issues – meet and discuss areas where your boss may need to become involved.

Your goal is to create or exceed expectations!

PARACHUTE QUESTIONS

When you enter or are responsible for a new group or situation

Always do an audit to find your base-line of performance and current results. In that way you can measure progress along the way, but also define the metrics of results at the end.

In addition, these Parachute Questions are a sighting on your environment, objectives, requirements, and personal strategy.

1. What is the **environment** like?

- What is the essential mission of the organization? Are there critical variables? (3 - 6 max)
- What assumption is the function operating on, within the organization?
- What are the key **inputs** (resources)? In what form does "work" come to you?
- What are the key **throughputs** (the process or steps to get things done internally)?
- What are the key **outputs** of the function? What does it look like when finished?
- What external forces impact the unit's performance?
- What are the critical performance standards? How do you know you're successful?
- What is an acceptable deviation from standard performance? Flexibility?
- What are the key performance indicators? What's your "wiggle room"?
- What are the controllable variables?
- What are the uncontrollable variables?
- How are resources controlled that are critical to your success?

2. What are your **business objectives** and **expected results**?

- What is your mission in your function? How does it fit into the organization?
- What is critical that you must personally do or not do?
- What are the key resources that you cannot do without? Which are solid?
- What are key indicators of your performance?
- What should it look like if it were perfect? Where is it now? What is the gap?

3. What should your **personal strategy** be?

- What will get you fired?
- What will get you promoted?
- How do you identify and get the information you need? How do you test its reliability?
- Who is the "client"? How much feedback to your boss? How often? In what form?
- In what form are the resources required for success?
- What changes do you need to negotiate with your boss to increase performance?
- What changes or upgrades or enhancements with your subordinates?
- What negotiated changes are possible with peers to increase your/their results?
- What external forces affect your strategy or results?
- What key information do you need to learn quickly? How do you get it?
- How do you identify diminishing returns? (time/energy going in versus results coming out)
- How should you allocate your time between priorities, resources and "all other"?

CHAPTER 16 - REAL-LIFE STORIES FOR INSIGHT AND AMUSEMENT

All of these "stories" are true and come from current or past clients

A "ROOKIE" MISTAKE: NEVER GIVE THE GAME AWAY!

Situation: I was interviewing for a Director's job with the Vice-President of a major NYC corporation. The interview was going well when he asked me: "We have a similar problem that you seem to have found a solution. How did you accomplish those results?"

What did I do wrong?: I answered the question, in exhaustive detail. I noticed that he took copious notes during my half-hour soliloquy as I laid out a detailed strategy. I should have answered the question with "WHAT" I did, and not detailed "HOW" I did it.

Results: I didn't get the job even though I was sure I hit a home run in the interview. A year later, I found out that he took "my plan", hired someone junior and told him to implement it. Of course, one can never take someone else's plan and make it succeed. I learned a very good lesson however. Never give away the total answer, only outline the steps.

WHAT NOT TO WEAR: FROM A HIGH LEVEL CORPORATE EXECUTIVE.

Situation: I was interviewing candidates for a career-launching marketing position in our footwear company. As expected, all of the candidates interviewed and dressed well.

Who didn't get the job? One candidate came to the interview wearing a competitor's shoes. They were unaware of the sensitivity of the mistake. It was like an "in your face" insult.

Who got the job? The finalist candidate not only wore our brand of shoe, but also impressed me with their research about footwear styles, competition, pricing, branding and vendor issues.

The moral of the story is that you're always on stage and even little things such as wearing the wrong shoes can unknowingly end your candidacy.

LISTEN CAREFULLY – A FAILURE TO COMMUNICATE

Situation: I had an interview for a mid-level position with a large retail food store chain. The interview was going well until, I realized later, I misunderstood a very simple but crucial question. The question was "What does customer service mean to our company?" What I heard was "How important is quality customer service to our company?" I wasn't listening.

What happened: I went on to answer the question that wasn't asked: I fully answered about the rise in the number of gourmet supermarkets, the need to compete on differentiation through customer service and not to compete on price. I listed other strategic reasons and thought that I had nailed the question. The interviewer gave me a bit of a confused look and I should have stopped and said, "Did I understand the question correctly", but didn't. After leaving the interview I realized that what she meant was simply - "What types of customer services do we currently offer that are most important to us?" I knew the answer to this simple question because I was a current customer. They always throw out fruits and vegetables that are less than perfect, offer the newest products and have a lot of attendants for customer service.

Results: I blew it! The lesson, of course, is what we all know but easily forget. If there is ANY ambiguity about a question always ask for a clarification. Most importantly though, be careful of trying to impress with complex answers, as insightful as they may be. TAKE YOUR TIME. Process each question before beginning your answer and repeat the question in your mind before answering. Make sure that you completely understand the question being asked of you. Confusion about a question is not intentional on their part. They want to hear you create and articulate an answer to the question they're asking, not a question you think they want to hear.

INTERVIEW SUCCESS – REDIRECTING A QUESTION

Situation: I was interviewing for a Director's job with the President of a high growth service business, with about 25 field offices in the Mid-West. He asked me to outline my current experiences and relate them to the job being offered.

How did I respond?: Quote: "My current position is with a consumer products company with flat growth, but it's not a service business. However, my prior company was a service business with 225 branches across the country. Your growth projections take you from 25 field offices to 150, nationally. Would it be of greater value to outline those parallel experiences first?"

Results: I got the job and in one year was named Vice President. The business accelerated across the country. I doubt I would have gotten the job if I had answered the President's original question without giving him an alternative.

A MISSED OPPORTUNITY: TAKE NOTHING FOR GRANTED

Situation: A colleague resigned making the internal job of my dreams available. I was thrilled to have the opportunity to move up. Little did I know that I was considered a really good fit and would be interviewed in the same week.

What did I do? I interviewed from the heart: How important this opportunity was for me, how my academic and professional experience meshed with the job requirements, the great value I could bring to the company, and so on. However, I did not have an updated resume and I didn't provide measurable results. I hadn't understood the challenges of the job, nor did I ask about expectations for that position. I spoke from the heart and not the brain, and wasn't prepared.

Results: A month later, I found out that I didn't get the job. Why? I assumed that they knew me and my work, that I was a shoo-in and I didn't have to research the position nor present my results as a candidate. Lesson: Never make assumptions.

ARE YOU CONNECTING WITH INTERVIEWERS? LEARN TO "READ" THEM.

Situation: I had just completed My Greener Future sessions # 6 and 7 on interviewing with my coach, practicing the skills that were taught, when I received a phone call requesting an interview with an executive at a high growth company. The changes we made to my resume were successful. I'm now getting an interview.

What I did differently: Before, I would have interviewed in my normal way, "selling" my abilities and competence. I now had a new set of skills I put to use. I assessed and "read" the style of the interviewer, then applied it to the "profile" of the job opening. I increased his comfort zone, identified the issues, and then applied alternative solutions to his business needs.

Results: Instead of a 15-minute cursory meeting, the interview became a 90-minute strategy session as to possible marketing approaches for new products. As I "bonded" with the executive, using the new interview approach, I now became a valued collaborator who was able to add substance to the discussion. At the end of the interview he apologized for having to cut the meeting short, but wanted me to return and discuss the job opening further.

GOOD BUSINESS "MANNERS" HELP TO GET THE JOB. ALWAYS FOLLOW THROUGH.

Situation: I had advanced to the final meeting for a director position, but blew the final interview because I had recently experienced a death in the family. I should have postponed the appointment, but I accepted the meeting even though emotionally numb.

What happened: During that final interview I was unable to demonstrate the chutzpah I had previously; my responses were lackluster. They hired another candidate who was more energetic. When I emerged from my lull, I committed to myself to optimize every job search – even the rejections – by expanding my social media connections with all my rejecters. I electronically linked with the executives and thanked them for considering me and wished them well in their endeavors (in addition to the traditional hand-written, hand stamped notes.

Results: When the other candidate did not show the same level of enthusiasm once hired, as when interviewed, they offered me a higher-level job! My communications savvy and creative approach to rejection made an impression on them. Morale: Always follow through, even if you come in second.

CHAPTER 17 – TESTIMONIALS

A number of past and current clients of My Greener Future, who have received one-on-one personalized and tailored-coaching sessions, have volunteered to assess the value they have received from participating in the program. Their words are conveyed here. 91% of all clients either have higher level jobs, been promoted within their own companies or are interviewing with highly interested corporations.

Here are their words:

"Bill Kaufmann and My Greener Future change my life!"

" I would not be leading my own company without it! " (An Entrepreneur, now President of a high growth direct sales Company)

" My Greener Future was an enormous help at the start of my career. " A Retail Sales person shifting to a Buyer Position for a National Retailer)

"I have a better picture of my true value and how to use my past accomplishments to leverage new alternatives. " (Operations Director, National non-profit, & Performance Consultant)

" I highly recommend this program to anyone in a career change or job market. " (Director of Marketing, a national Merchandising & Distribution company)

Quotes:

- **"Outstanding program that I would recommend to anyone", Pat M, Ohio**

- **"I thought I knew how to market myself. I didn't. My resume went from blah to eye-popping!" Rich K, Virginia**

- **"Bill saw my future before I did. I'm currently achieving my dream!"...Mary in Ohio**

- **"My Greener Future helped me enter a new and exciting career direction" Chris in Jacksonville, Florida**

- **"You can pay someone to find you a job, but individualized coaching on the art of marketing yourself.... Priceless." Ken A., Chesterfield, Va.**

- **"My Greener Future gave me a direction that changed my life"
Sharon R., Salt Lake City, Utah**

CHAPTER 18 - MOVING FROM THIS HANDBOOK TO COACHING

The purpose of this handbook is to overview the stages and steps in a job search strategy for those who can translate this material into action. Most people needing assistance prefer to have a professional expert work with them in a step-by-step process. In this way, you have a mentor to not only help provide the strategies to your tailor-made, custom designed plan, but also to help you practice new skills and experiences for you to use.

Utilizing a professional mentor provides the support that gives you an advantage among your peer competitors who are searching for the same positions that you are in a crowded marketplace. It's the edge that will make the difference.

Bill Kaufmann, President, My Greener Future

Mygreenerfuture1@cox.net   Mygreenerfuture.com

REFERENCES

Purple Squirrel is a book by that name written by Michael Junge

Made in the USA
Columbia, SC
26 August 2018